中英对照

青草中英双语分级读物

# 幽默故事

第2级

总主编 林梅

本书主编 孙清莹

幽默是人们智慧的凝聚

让我们笑着面对生活

北京航空航天大学出版社
BEIHANG UNIVERSITY PRESS

**图书在版编目（CIP）数据**

幽默故事：汉英对照 / 林梅，孙清莹主编 . -- 北京：北京航空航天大学出版社，2016.5

（青青草中英双语分级读物 / 林梅主编 . 第 2 级）

ISBN 978-7-5124-2081-6

Ⅰ. ①幽…　Ⅱ. ① 林…　② 孙…　Ⅲ. ①英语 - 汉语 - 对照读物　②故事 - 作品集 - 世界　Ⅳ. ① H319.4：I

中国版本图书馆 CIP 数据核字（2016）第 056400 号



**青青草中英双语分级读物——幽默故事（第2级）**

总主编　林　梅

本书主编　孙清莹

责任编辑　秦　莹

*

北京航空航天大学出版社出版发行

北京市海淀区学院路 37 号（邮编 100191）　http://www.buaapress.com.cn

发行部电话：（010）82317024　传真：（010）82328026

读者信箱：bhyaiyu@163.com　邮购电话：（010）82316936

北京佳信达欣艺术印刷有限公司印装　各地书店经销

*

开本：787×1092　1/32　印张：9.75　字数：319 千字

2017 年 1 月第 1 版　2017 年 1 月第 1 次印刷

ISBN 978-7-5124-2081-6　定价：29.80 元

---

若本书有倒页、脱页、缺页等印装质量问题，请与本社发行部联系调换。联系电话：（010）82317024

# 编委会

# 前　言

语言表达能力的好坏主要靠词汇量的积累，而词汇量的积累最主要的途径是阅读。研究表明：美国儿童的阅读量是中国儿童的六倍。所以想要英语好，阅读是不可忽略的关键因素。

《青青草中英双语分级读物》是一套适合小学到大学的分级阅读材料，整个套系选材考究、内容丰富多样，涵盖了童话、寓言、歌曲、电影、小说、演讲等题材，能帮助您从培养兴趣开始，循序渐进，一步一步地把您带入英语的殿堂。

配有外教真人原声录制的音频，可让您在阅读之余练习听力和跟读，也可让您进行复述、提炼和总结。这是一套能帮助您提高语言发展、阅读能力、写作能力等综合训练的工具。

这套读物的教育意义不靠说教，不靠灌输，而是渗透式、启发式的，让您在愉悦的阅读过程中学习语言、爱上阅读，并为将来的写作奠定基础。

编者

2016 年于北京

# 目 录

# Big Head
# 大脑袋

1 “All the kids make fun of me,” the boy cried to his mother. “They say I have a big head.”

2 “Don't listen to them,” his mother comforted him. “You have a beautiful head. Now stop crying and go to the store for ten pounds of potatoes.”

3 “Where's the shopping bag?”

4 “I haven't got one. Use your hat.”

## 点睛译文

1 小男孩哭着跟妈妈说：“所有的孩子都拿我开玩笑，他们说我长了个大脑袋。”

2 他妈妈就安慰他：“别听他们的，你的脑袋长得很漂亮啊。好了，别哭了，去商店买10磅土豆来。”

3 “购物袋在哪儿呢？”

4 “我没有购物袋，就用你的帽子吧。”

## 生词宝库

comfort [ˈkʌmfət] *v.* 安慰

pound [paʊnd] *n.* 磅（1磅约等于0.454千克）

potato [pəˈteɪtəʊ] *n.* 土豆

shopping [ˈʃɒpɪŋ] *n.* 购物

# Two Pieces of Cake
# 两块蛋糕

## 点睛译文

1 汤姆：妈妈，我可以吃两块蛋糕吗？

2 妈妈：当然可以——拿这块蛋糕把它切成两块吧！

## 爆笑故事

1 Tom: Mom, can I have two pieces of cake, please?

2 Mom: Certainly – take this piece and cut it two!

## 生词宝库

piece [piːs] *n.* 块

cake [keɪk] *n.* 蛋糕

certainly [ˈsɜːtnlɪ] *adv.* 当然

cut [kʌt] *v.* 切

# A Gentle Reminder
# 委婉提醒

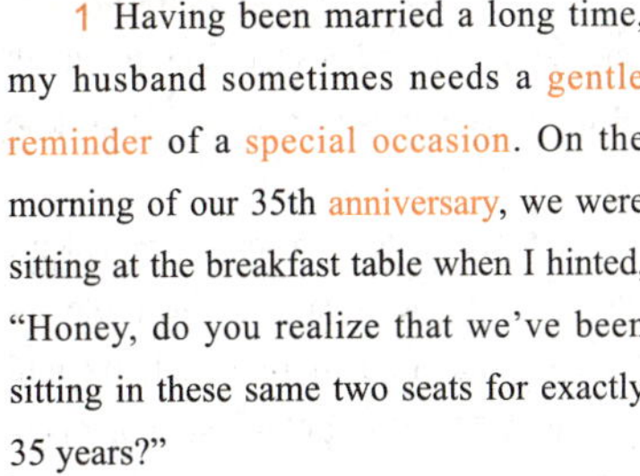

## 爆笑故事

1 Having been married a long time, my husband sometimes needs a gentle reminder of a special occasion. On the morning of our 35th anniversary, we were sitting at the breakfast table when I hinted, “Honey, do you realize that we’ve been sitting in these same two seats for exactly 35 years?”

2 Putting down the newspaper, he looked straight at me and said, “So, you want to switch seats?”

## 点睛译文

1 婚后已久，我丈夫却经常忘记那些特殊的值得纪念的日子，往往需要委婉的提醒。在我们结婚35周年纪念日的早上，我们正坐在早餐桌旁，我暗示道：“亲爱的，你意识到我们在这两个相同的座位上已坐了整整35年了吗？”

2 他放下报纸，眼睛直直地望着我说：“所以，你是想交换座位吗？”

## 生词宝库

gentle [ˈdʒentl] *adj.* 温和的

reminder [rɪˈmaɪndə] *n.* 暗示

special [ˈspeʃəl] *adj.* 特别的

occasion [əˈkeɪʒn] *n.* 时刻

anniversary [ˌænɪˈvɜːsərɪ] *n.* 周年纪念

straight [streɪt] *adv.* 直接

# A Dollar Per Point

# 一分一块钱

## 爆笑故事

1 A professor was giving a big test one day to his students. He handed out all of the tests and went back to his desk to wait.

2 Once the test was over, the students all handed the tests back in. The professor noticed that one of the students had attached a $100 bill to his test with a note saying, "A dollar per point."

3 The next class the professor handed the tests back out. This student got back his test and $64 change.

## 点睛译文

1 一天，教授正在给学生们监考。他发下试卷，然后回到讲台前等待。

2 考试结束了，学生们纷纷交回试卷。教授发现一张试卷上别着一张百元钞票，还有一张纸条，上面写着："一分一块钱。"

3 第二堂课，教授把试卷都发回学生们手中。其中一个学生不但得到了试卷，还得到了 64 块钱的找零。

## 生词宝库

test [test] *n.* 测试

wait [weɪt] *v.* 等待

hand [hænd] *v.* 交给

notice [ˈnəʊtɪs] *v.* 注意

attach [əˈtætʃ] *v.* 附

bill [bɪl] *n.* 钞票

point [pɒɪnt] *n.* 得分

change [tʃeɪndʒ] *n.* 找零

# How Much English Can You Speak 你会说多少英文

## 爆笑故事

1 "Your Honor, I want to bring to your attention how unfair it is for my client to be accused of theft. He arrived in New York City a week ago and barely knew his way around. What's more, he only speaks a few words of English."

2 The judge looked at the defendant and asked, "How much English can you speak?"

3 The defendant looked up and said, "Give me your wallet!"

## 点睛译文

1 "法官先生，我的当事人被指控偷窃，这是多么不公正啊。他一周前才来到纽约，几乎都不认路。而且，他只会说几个英语单词。"

2 法官看了看被告，问道："你会说多少英文？"

3 被告抬起头，说："把你的钱包给我！"

## 生词宝库

attention [ə'tenʃən] *n.* 注意力

unfair [ˌʌn'feə] *adj.* 不公平的

client ['klaɪənt] *n.* 客户

barely ['beəlɪ] *adv.* 几乎不

judge [dʒʌdʒ] *n.* 法官

defendant [dɪ'fendənt] *n.* 被告

# Women Talk More than Men 女人比男人啰嗦

点睛译文

1 丈夫给妻子看了一项调查结果，以向她证明女人比男人啰嗦。研究表明，男人平均每天使用15,000个字，而女人每天使用30,000个。

2 妻子想了一会儿说，女人每天说的字数是男人的两倍，因为她们必须重复已经说过的话。

3 他问："什么？"

爆笑故事

1 A husband, proving to his wife that women talk more than men, showed her a study which indicated that men use on average only 15,000 words a day, whereas women use 30,000 words a day.

2 She thought about this for a while and then told her husband that women use twice as many words as men because they have to repeat everything they say.

3 He said, "What?"

生词宝库

wife [waɪf] *n.* 妻子

indicate [ˈɪndɪkeɪt] *v.* 表明

average [ˈævərɪdʒ] *n.* 平均；平均水平

whereas [ˌweərˈæz] *conj.* 然而

twice [twaɪs] *adv.* 两倍

repeat [rɪˈpiːt] *v.* 重复

# Is This Seat Empty
# 这个座位是空着的吗

1 Boy: Is this seat empty?

2 Girl: Yes, and this one will be if you sit down.

1 男孩：这个座位是空着的吗？

2 女孩：是的，如果你坐下，我的座位也将是空着的。

seat [siːt] *n.* 座位
empty ['emptɪ] *adj.* 空的
sit [sɪt] *v.* 坐

# My Brother Is Crying
# 我弟弟在哭

## 点睛译文

1 妈妈在厨房里问："汤姆，你弟弟怎么了？他在哭。"

2 汤姆答道："哦，没事儿，妈妈。我在吃我的蛋糕。他哭是因为我不给他吃。"

3 "他已经吃完自己的了吗？"

4 "是的。"汤姆说，"我帮他吃完时，他也哭了。"

## 爆笑故事

1 "Tom, what's the matter with your brother?" asked the mother in the kitchen. "He's crying."

2 "Oh, nothing, Mum," replied Tom, "I'm eating my cake. He is crying because I won't give him any."

3 "But has he finished his own cake?"

4 "Yes." said Tom. "And he also cried when I was helping him finish that."

## 生词宝库

matter [ˈmætə] *n.* 问题
because [bɪˈkɒz] *conj.* 因为；由于
finish [ˈfɪnɪʃ] *v.* 吃完，吃光
cry [kraɪ] *v.* 哭

# How Many Coins
# 有几枚硬币

## 爆笑故事

1 A guy says to his friend, "Guess how many coins I have in my pocket."

2 The friend says, "If I guess right, will you give me one of them?"

3 The first guy says, "If you guess right, I'll give you both of them!"

## 点睛译文

1 一个人对他的朋友说："猜猜我兜里有几个子儿？"

2 他的朋友说："我猜对了，你能给我一个不？"

3 这个人就说："你要猜对了，我两个全都给你！"

## 生词宝库

guy [gaɪ] *n.* 家伙；（男）人

coin [kɒɪn] *n.* 硬币

pocket [ˈpɒkɪt] *n.* 口袋

friend [frend] *n.* 朋友

both [bəʊθ] *pron.* 两者

# Graduate and Undergraduate
# 研究生与本科生

1 一名教师在研究生工程学课堂上说："我一眼就能看出来哪些是本科生，哪些是研究生。我说'下午好'的时候，本科生回答'下午好'；而研究生则会把这句话记在本子上。"

1 "I can always tell a graduate class from an undergraduate class," said an instructor at a university graduate engineering course. "When I say 'Good afternoon', the undergraduates respond 'Good afternoon'. But the graduate students just write it down."

graduate [ˈɡrædʒʊət] *adj.* <美>研究生的，研究院的；研究生

undergraduate [ˌʌndəˈɡrædʒʊət] *adj.* 大学生的；*n.* 本科生

instructor [ɪnˈstrʌktə] *n.* 教师

engineering [ˌendʒɪˈnɪərɪŋ] *n.* 工程学

# Making Faces
# 做鬼脸

## 爆笑故事

1 Finding one of her students making faces at others on the playground, Ms. Smith stopped to gently reprimand the child.

2 Smiling sweetly, the Sunday school teacher said, "Bobby, when I was a child I was told if I made ugly faces, my face would freeze and stay like that."

3 Bobby looked up and replied, "Well, Ms. Smith, you can't say you weren't warned."

## 点睛译文

1 史密斯小姐发现她的一名学生在操场上冲别人做鬼脸，便去轻责他。

2 这位主日学校的老师甜甜地微笑着，说："博比，我小的时候，有人警告我说如果我做鬼脸，我的脸就会僵硬，然后永远都会那么丑。"

3 博比抬头看了看老师，说："那个，史密斯小姐，你可别说没人警告过你啊。"

## 生词宝库

make face *v.* 做鬼脸

playground [ˈpleɪgraʊnd] *n.* 操场

reprimand [ˈreprɪmɑːnd] *v.* 训斥

freeze [friːz] *v.* 僵硬

warn [wɔːn] *vt.* 警告

# Thanks for the Peanuts

# 谢谢您的花生

## 点睛译文

1 一名男子带着朋友去探望他的祖母。

2 他和祖母聊天时，他的朋友开始吃咖啡桌上放的花生，并把花生都给吃光了。

3 他们离开时，他的朋友对祖母说："谢谢您的花生。"

4 结果祖母说："唉！自从我牙齿掉光后，我就只能吮掉花生豆外层的巧克力了。"

## 爆笑故事

1 A guy goes to visit his grandma and he brings his friend with him.

2 While he's talking to his grandma, his friend starts eating the peanuts on the coffee table, and finishes them off.

3 As they're leaving, his friend says to his grandma, "Thanks for the peanuts."

4 She says, "Yeah, since I lost my dentures I can only suck the chocolate off."

## 生词宝库

peanut [ˈpiːnʌt] *n.* 花生

coffee [ˈkɒfɪ] *n.* 咖啡

table [ˈteɪbəl] *n.* 桌子

denture [ˈdentʃə] *n.* 假牙

suck [sʌk] *v.* 吸吮

# You Will Not Have Worms

# 肚子里就不会长虫子

1 A father was trying to teach his son the evils of alcohol.

2 He put one worm in a glass of water and another worm in a glass of whiskey. The worm in the water lived, while the one in the whiskey curled up and died.

3 "All right, son," asked the father, "What does that show you?"

4 "Well, Dad, it shows that if you drink alcohol, you will not have worms."

1 一位父亲打算让自己的儿子知道酒精有多么可怕。

2 他分别把两只虫子放到一杯清水和一杯威士忌里做对比。清水里虫子安然无恙，结果威士忌里的虫子蜷缩了几下就死掉了。

3 父亲问道："好了，儿子啊，你得出了什么结论？"

4 "嗯，爸爸，这说明，你只要喝酒的话，肚里就不会长虫了！"

evil [ˈiːvl] *n.* 弊病

alcohol [ˈælkəhɒl] *n.* 酒精

worm [wɜːm] *n.* 虫，蠕虫

whiskey [ˈwɪskɪ] *n.* 威士忌酒

curl [kɜːl] *v.* 弯曲

# I Didn't Need the Money Then 我那时还不缺钱

## 点睛译文

1 一个穷人走进大夫的诊室，他看起来很不舒服。

2 他说："大夫！ 帮帮我！一个月前我吞了个一分的硬币！"

3 大夫说："天啊，早干嘛去了？你当时怎么不来看？"

4 穷人回答："实话告诉您吧，大夫，我当时还没那么缺钱！"

## 爆笑故事

1 Looking very unhappy, a poor man entered a doctor's consulting-room.

2 "Doctor," he said, "you must help me. I swallowed a penny about a month ago."

3 "Good heavens, man!" said the doctor. "Why have you waited so long? Why don't you come to me on the day you swallowed it?"

4 "To tell you the truth, Doctor," the poor man replied, "I didn't need the money so badly then."

## 生词宝库

unhappy [ʌnˈhæpɪ] *adj.* 不快乐的

consulting-room [kənˈsʌltɪŋrʊm] *n.* 诊室

swallow [ˈswɒləʊ] *v.* 吞下

penny [ˈpenɪ] *n.*（美）分；便士

truth [truːθ] *n.* 事实

# I Never Make the Same Mistake Twice
# 我从不犯两次同样的错误

1 Boy: Hi, didn't we go on dates before? Once or twice?

2 Girl: Must've been once. I never make the same mistake twice.

1 男孩：嗨，我们之前是不是约会过？是一次还是两次来着？

2 女孩：应该只有一次。同样的错误我从不犯两次。

## 生词宝库

date [deɪt] *n.* 约会
once [wʌns] *n.* 一次
twice [twaɪs] *adv.* 两次
never [ˈnevə] *adv.* 永不
mistake [mɪˈsteɪk] *n.* 错误

# Quality of a Musician
# 音乐家的素质

1 在一次音乐学院的入学考试中，老师问其中一个男孩："音乐家最重要的生理素质是什么？"

2 "耳聋。"男孩答道。

3 "胡说！"老师气愤地说。

4 男孩轻蔑地反问道："怎么了，先生！难道您不知道大名鼎鼎的音乐家贝多芬是个聋子吗？"

1 In an entrance examination of a conservatory of music, a teacher asked one of the boys, "What is the most important physiological quality of a musician?"

2 "To be deaf." replied the boy.

3 "Nonsense!" said the teacher angrily.

4 "Why, sir! Don't you know that the famous musician Beethoven was deaf?" the boy asked in reply disdainfully.

## 生词宝库

entrance [ˈentrəns] *n.* 入学

examination [ɪɡˌzæmɪˈneɪʃən] *n.* 考试

conservatory [kənˈsɜːvətrɪ] *n.* 音乐学院

physiological [ˌfɪzɪəˈlɒdʒɪkl] *adj.* 生理的

quality [ˈkwɒlɪtɪ] *n.* 特质；质量

musician [mjuːˈzɪʃn] *n.* 音乐家

deaf [def] *adj.* 聋的

disdainfully [dɪsˈdeɪnfʊlɪ] *adv.* 轻蔑地

# The Month Is Up Today

# 今天是一个月的最后一天

## 爆笑故事

1 (A man sat at a bar, had the saddest hangdog expression.)

2 Bartender: What's the matter? Are you having troubles with your wife?

3 The man: We had a fight, and she told me that she wasn't going to speak to me for a month.

4 Bartender: That should make you happy.

5 The man: No, the month is up today!

## 点睛译文

1（一个男人坐在酒吧里，伤心至极。）

2 酒保：你怎么了？跟老婆闹矛盾了？

3 男人：我们吵了一架，她说一个月都不会跟我说话。

4 酒保：那你应该高兴才是啊！

5 男人：不，今天是这个月的最后一天！

## 生词宝库

hangdog [ˈhæŋdɒg] *adj.* 忧愁的，悲哀的

expression [ɪkˈspreʃn] *n.* 表情

fight [faɪt] *n.* 打架

month [mʌnθ] *n.* 月

# How Much for a Season
# 一个季度多少钱

点睛译文

1 女生宿舍将全面禁止男生进入，男生宿舍也同样不得女生光临。

2 “不论是谁，一旦发现违规，初犯将被罚款20美元。再犯要被罚款60美元。第3次被抓需要交180美元的罚款。还有什么疑问吗？”

3 这时人群中一个男同学问道，“嗯……那么一个季度的通行证需要多少钱？”

1 The female dormitory will be out-of-bounds for all male students and vice versa.

2 “Anybody caught breaking this rule will be fined $20 the first time. Anybody caught breaking this rule the second time will be fined $60. Being caught a third time will incur a fine of $180. Are there any questions?”

3 At this moment, a male student in the crowd inquires, “Umm... How much for a season pass?”

生词宝库

female [ˈfi:meɪl] *adj.* 女性的

dormitory [ˈdɔ:mɪtərɪ] *n.* 宿舍

male [meɪl] *adj.* 男性的

vice versa [ˌvaɪsˈvɜ:sə] *adv.* 反过来也是一样地

rule [ru:l] *n.* 规则

fine [faɪn] *v.* 罚款

incur [ɪnˈkɜ:] *v.* 招致

inquire [ɪnˈkwaɪə] *v.* 询问

# Can I Buy You a Drink

# 我能给你买杯饮料吗

1 Boy: Can I buy you a drink?

2 Girl: Actually I'd rather have the money.

1 男孩：我可以给你买杯饮料吗？

2 女孩：你不如直接把钱给我得了。

生词宝库

buy [baɪ] *v.* 买

drink [drɪŋk] *n.* 饮料

rather [ˈrɑːðə] *adv.* 倒不如

money [ˈmʌnɪ] *n.* 钱

# Falling
# 坠落

1 皮特：我上次出去打猎，从很高的悬崖上跌了下来，信不信由你，当我跌落的时候，我脑海里浮现了我做过的所有蠢事。

2 鲍勃：你一定是从万丈高山上跌落的吧。

1 Peter: The last time I was out hunting, I stepped off a high cliff, and would you believe it, while I was falling every fool deed I'd ever done came into my mind.

2 Bob: Must have been a pretty high mountain you fell from.

hunting [ˈhʌntɪŋ] *n.* 打猎

step off 跌落

cliff [klɪf] *n.* 悬崖

fool [fuːl] *n.* 傻瓜

deed [diːd] *n.* 行动

mountain [ˈmaʊntən] *n.* 山

# God Isn't Deaf
# 上帝不聋

## 爆笑故事

1 Spending the night with their grandparents, two young boys knelt beside their beds to say their prayers at bedtime. The younger boy began praying at the top of his lungs, "I pray for a bike... I pray for a new DVD..."

2 His older brother nudged him and said, "Why are you shouting your prayers? God isn't deaf."

3 To which the little brother replied, "No, but Grandma is!"

## 点睛译文

1 两个男孩与祖父母一起过夜，他们跪在床边做睡前祷告。弟弟声嘶力竭地祈祷："我祈求一辆自行车……我祈求一张新的DVD……"

2 哥哥用肘轻推他："你为什么大喊着祈祷？上帝又不聋。"

3 弟弟答道："上帝是不聋，但是奶奶聋。"

## 生词宝库

spend [spend] v. 度过

grandparents [ˈgrændpeərənts] n. 祖父母，外祖父母

knee [niː] v. 跪着

pray [preɪ] v. 祈祷

lung [lʌŋ] n. 肺

nudge [nʌdʒ] v. 用肘轻推

# Goethe's Tolerance

# 歌德的容忍

1 一次，歌德正在魏玛一个公园的一条狭窄小道上散步。碰巧他遇见一个对他怀有敌意的评论家。两人都停了下来，彼此相互对视。然后评论家说道：“我从来不给傻瓜让路。”

2 “可我给。”说完歌德退到了一边。

1 Goethe was once strolling on a narrow path in a park in Weimar. As luck would have it, he met with a critic who was hostile to him. Both of them stopped, staring at each other. Then the critic said, “I'll never make way for a fool.”

2 “But I will,” with that Goethe retreated aside.

## 生词宝库

stroll [strəʊl] *v.* 漫步

critic [ˈkrɪtɪk] *n.* 评论家

hostile [ˈhɒstaɪl] *adj.* 敌对的

retreat [rɪˈtriːt] *v.* 后退

# Cat and Mice

# 猫和老鼠

## 爆笑故事

1 Mrs Brown went to visit one of her friend and carried a small box with holes punched in the top.

2 "What's in your box?" asked the friend.

3 "A cat," answered Mrs. Brown. "You see I've been dreaming about mice at night and I'm so scared! This cat is to catch them."

4 "But the mice are only imaginary," said the friend.

5 "So is the cat," whispered Mrs. Brown.

## 点睛译文

1 布朗夫人去拜访一位朋友，她拿着一个顶部扎满了小眼儿的盒子。

2 "盒子里装的是什么？"朋友问道。

3 "一只小猫，"布朗夫人回答说，"你知道我晚上睡觉总梦见老鼠，我非常害怕。这只猫可以抓住那些老鼠。"

4 "可老鼠都是假想的呀。"朋友说。

5 "小猫也是假想的。"布朗夫人小声说道。

## 生词宝库

hole [həʊl] *v.* 挖洞

punch [pʌntʃ] *v.* 开洞

mice [maɪs] *n.* 老鼠（mouse 的复数）

scared [skeəd] *adj.* 害怕的

imaginary [ɪ'mædʒɪnərɪ] *adj.* 想象的

# Reached Shore Fast

# 快速靠岸

## 点睛译文

1 在休伦湖钓完鱼后，我的一个朋友开车拖着他的船回家，结果路上车坏了。他没带手机，不过，他想，也许他可以通过海事无线广播来请求公路援助。于是，他爬到他的船里面，启动了无线装置，喊道："求救，求救。"

2 一名海岸护卫队警官作出了回应："报告你的位置。"

3 "I-75 号公路，斯坦迪什的南面两英里。"沉默了好一会之后，警官问我的朋友："你的船靠岸时开得有多快？"

## 爆笑故事

1 A guy I know was towing his boat home from a fishing trip to Lake Huron when his car broke down. He didn't have his cell phone with him, but he thought maybe he might be able to raise someone on his marine radio to call for roadside assistance. He climbed into his boat, clicked on the radio and said, "Mayday, mayday."

2 A Coast Guard officer came on and said, "State your location."

3 "I-75, two miles south of Standish." After a very long pause, the officer asked, "How fast were you going when you reached shore?"

## 生词宝库

tow [təʊ] *v.* 拖

raise [reɪz] *v.* 将（某事物）引起注意

marine [mə'riːn] *adj.* 船舶的

assistance [ə'sɪstəns] *n.* 援助

click [klɪk] *v.* 点击

pause [pɔːz] *v.* 停顿

# On St. Peter
# 圣彼德的问题

1 Three men, a doctor, an accountant and a lawyer are dead and they appear in front of St. Peter. St. Peter tells them that they have to answer one question in order to get to Heaven.

2 He looks at the doctor and asks, "There was a movie that was made about a ship that sank after hitting an iceberg. What was its name?"

3 The doctor answers, "*The Titanic*." And he is sent through.

4 He then looks at the accountant and say, "How many people died in that ship?"

5 Fortunately the accountant had just watched the movie and he answers, "1500!"

6 St. Peter sends him through and then finally turns to the lawyer and commands,

点睛译文

1 有3个人死了，分别是一名医生、一名会计和一名律师。他们来到了圣彼德面前。圣彼德对他们说，如果他们想进入天堂，就得每人回答一个问题。

2 圣彼德看着医生开始发问："以前电影院放过一部电影，说的是一艘船撞击冰山后沉没，电影的名字是什么？"

3 医生回答："《泰坦尼克号》。"医生随即被允许进入天堂。

4 然后圣彼德看着会计说："船上有多少人遇难？"

5 会计很走运，因为他刚看过这部电影，回答道："1500人遇难。"

6 圣彼德把会计也放进天堂了。最后，圣彼德转过

身，看着律师，非常严肃地用命令的口吻问道："把 1500 人的名字都说出来。"

in a very heavy voice, "Name them!"

accountant [əˈkaʊntənt] *n.* 会计师

lawyer [ˈlɔːjə] *n.* 律师

iceberg [ˈaɪsbɜːg] *n.* 冰山

command [kəˈmɑːnd] *v.* 命令

# Blind Date

# 相亲

## 爆笑故事

1 After being with her all evening, the man couldn't take another minute with his blind date. Earlier, he had secretly arranged to have a friend call him to the phone so he would have an excuse to leave. When he returned to the table, he lowered his eyes, put on a grim expression and said, "I have some bad news. My grandfather just died."

2 "Thank heavens," his date replied. "If yours hadn't, mine would have had to!"

## 点睛译文

1 和相亲对象待了一晚上后，男人再也受不了了。他事先安排了个朋友给他打电话，这样他就能借故先离开了。当他回到桌边，他垂下眼睛，装出一副阴沉的表情，说："有个不幸的消息，我的祖父刚刚去世了。"

2 "谢天谢地！"他的约会对象说，"如果你的祖父不死，我的祖父就得死了！"

## 生词宝库

minute ['mɪnɪt] *n.* 片刻

blind date [blaɪnd deɪt] *n.* 相亲

secretly ['siːkrətlɪ] *adv.* 秘密地

arrange [ə'reɪndʒ] *v.* 安排

excuse [ɪk'skjuːz] *n.* 借口

grim [grɪm] *adj.* 阴冷的

# The Mean Man's Party

# 吝啬鬼的聚会

1 一个声名狼藉的小气鬼终于决定要请一次客了。他在向一个朋友解释怎么才能找到他家时说：“你上到5楼，用你的胳膊肘按门铃。门开了后，再用你的脚把门推开。”

2 “为什么我要用我的肘和脚呢？”

3 “天啊！”吝啬鬼回答，“你总不会空着手来吧？”

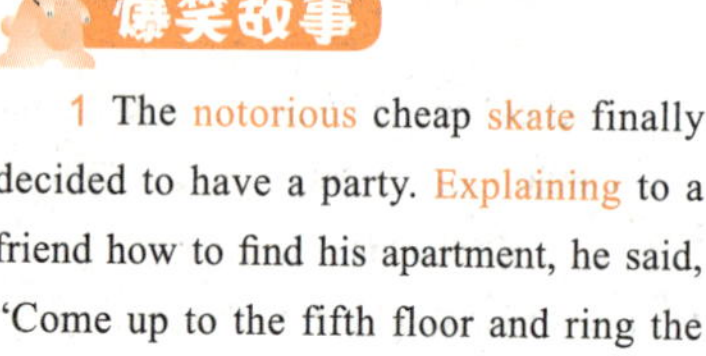

1 The notorious cheap skate finally decided to have a party. Explaining to a friend how to find his apartment, he said, “Come up to the fifth floor and ring the doorbell with your elbow. When the door opens, push with your foot.”

2 “Why use my elbow and foot?”

3 “Well, gosh,” was the reply, “You're not coming empty-handed, are you?”

## 生词宝库

notorious [nəʊˈtɔːrɪəs] *adj.* 臭名昭著的

skate [skeɪt] *n.* 家伙，人

explain [ɪkˈspleɪn] *v.* 说明；解释

doorbell [ˈdɔːbel] *n.* 门铃

elbow [ˈelbəʊ] *n.* 手肘

# Talking Clock
# 会说话的钟

## 爆笑故事

1 While proudly showing off his new apartment to friends, a college student led the way into the den.

2 "What is the big brass gong and hammer for?" one of his friends asked.

3 "That is the talking clock," the man replied.

4 "How does it work?"

5 "Watch," the man said and proceeded to give the gong an ear shattering pound with the hammer. Suddenly, someone screamed from the other side of the wall, "Knock it off, you idiot! It's two o'clock in the morning!"

## 点睛译文

1 一个学生带他的朋友们参观他的新公寓，甚是得意。

2 他的一个朋友问他："那个大铜锣和锤子是干什么用的？"

3 "那玩意儿厉害了，那是一个会说话的钟，"学生回答。

4 "这钟怎么工作的？"

5 "看着，别眨眼啊。"那学生走上前一把操起铜锣和锤子，拼命地敲了一下，声音震耳欲聋。突然，他们听到隔壁那边有人狂叫："别敲了，你这白痴！现在都凌晨两点钟了！"

## 生词宝库

show off 炫耀

apartment [əˈpɑːtmənt] *n.* 一套公寓房间

brass [brɑːs] *adj.* 黄铜的

shattering [ˈʃætərɪŋ] *adj.* 破碎的

hammer [ˈhæmə] *n.* 锤

# The Great Event

# 重大事件

## 点睛译文

1 老师：1809 年发生了什么重大事件？

2 小威利：亚伯拉罕·林肯诞生。

3 老师：正确。那么 1812 年发生了什么重要事件呢？

4 小威利：亚伯拉罕·林肯过他的 3 周岁生日。

## 爆笑故事

1 Teacher: What great event happened in 1809?

2 Little Willy: Abraham Lincoln was born.

3 Teacher: Correct. And what great event happened in 1812?

4 Little Willy: Abraham Lincoln had his third birthday.

## 词汇无障碍

event [ɪˈvent] *n.* 事件

correct [kəˈrekt] *adj.* 正确的

# Much Worse
# 更糟了

1 Policeman: Why didn't you shout for help when you were robbed of your watch?

2 Man: If I had opened my mouth, they'd have found my four gold teeth. That would be much worse.

## 点睛译文

1 警察：有人抢你的手表时，你为什么不呼救呢？

2 男子：要是我张口的话，他们就会发现我的4颗金牙。那就更糟了。

## 生词宝库

policeman [pəˈliːsmən] *n.*（男）警察

shout [ʃaʊt] *v.* 呼喊；高声呼叫

rob [rɒb] *v.* 抢劫

mouth [maʊθ] *n.* 口

gold [gəʊld] *adj.* 金的

teeth [tiːθ] *n.* 牙齿（tooth 的复数）

# Lines in Heaven
# 天堂里的队

## 点睛译文

1 世上的每一个人死后都上了天堂。

2 上帝说："要男人分成两队，一队是在世上控制女人的男人，另一队是被女人鞭打的男人。另外女子自成一队，跟着圣彼德去。"

3 队伍排列好后，有两个队伍。一队是被女人鞭打的，有100英里长；一队是在世上控制女人的，仅有一人。

4 上帝生气地说："你们男人应该感到羞耻，我按照自己的形象创造了你们，而你们却被女子鞭打。看看，我鹤立鸡群的唯一的儿子，他使我骄傲。你们应该向他学习！告诉他们，儿子，你如何成为唯一一个站在这一队上的人？"

5 这男子回答说："我不知道，我太太叫我站在这儿的。"

1 Everybody on earth dies and goes to heaven.

2 God comes and says: "I want the men to make two lines. One line is for the men that dominated their women on earth and the other line is for the men that were whipped by their women. Also, I want all the women to go with St. Peter."

3 Said and done, and there are two lines. The line of the men that were whipped was 100 miles long, and the line of men that dominated women, there was only one man.

4 God got mad and said: "You men should be ashamed of yourselves. I created you in my image and you were all whipped by your mates. Look at the only one of my sons that stood up and made me proud. Learn from him! Tell them, my son, how did you manage to be the only one on that line?"

5 The man said, "I don't know, my wife told me to stand here."

heaven ['hevn] *n.* 天堂

dominate ['dɒmɪneɪt] *v.* 支配

whip [wɪp] *v.* 抽打

ashamed [ə'ʃeɪmd] *adj.* 感到惭愧的

mate [meɪt] *n.* 配偶

manage ['mænɪdʒ] *v.* 设法

# Secret for a Long Life

# 长寿的秘诀

1 一位女士走向坐在门廊椅子上摇动着的小老头。

2 “我无意中发现，你是那么幸福，”那女士说。“你幸福而长寿的秘密是什么？”

3 “我每天抽 3 包烟，每周喝一箱威士忌，吃高脂肪食品，而且从来不曾锻炼过。”

4 “哦，真神奇，”女士说，“您高寿？”

5 “26。”

1 A woman walks up to a little old man rocking in a chair on his porch.

2 “I couldn’t help noticing how happy you look,” she says. “What’s your secret for a long, happy life?”

3 “I smoke three packs a day, drink a case of whiskey a week, eat fatty foods and never, ever exercise.”

4 “Wow, that’s amazing,” says the woman. “How old are you?”

5 “Twenty-six.”

## 生词宝库

rock [rɒk] *v.* 来回摇动

chair [tʃeə] *n.* 椅子

porch [pɔːtʃ] *n.* 门廊

smoke [sməʊk] *v.* 抽烟

pack [pæk] *n.* 一包

fatty [ˈfætɪ] *adj.* 多脂肪的

# Response Ability

# 答问技巧

1 An Ogden, Iowa, minister was matching coins with a member of his congregation for a cup of coffee. When asked if that didn't constitute gambling, the minister replied, "It's merely a scientific method of determining just who is going to commit an act of charity."

2 Philosopher Bertrand Russell, asked if he was willing to die for his beliers, replied: "Of course not. After all, I may be wrong."

3 A newspaper organized a contest for the best answer to the question: "If a fire broke out in the Louvre, and if you could only save one painting, which one would you carry out?"

4 The winning reply was: "The one nearest the exit."

点睛译文

1 爱荷华州奥格根的一位牧师正在与一位教友为一杯咖啡而猜硬币。别人问他那是否构成赌博行为时，牧师答道："这仅仅是决定由谁来做一件善事的一种科学方法。"

2 当有人问哲学家伯特兰·罗素是否愿意为了他的信仰而献身时，他答道："当然不会。毕竟，我可能会是错的。"

3 一家报社组织了一场竞赛，为下面的问题征集最佳答案："如果卢浮宫起了火，而你只能救出一幅画，你将救出哪一幅？"

4 获奖的答案是："最接近门口的那一幅。"

## 词汇无障碍

minister [ˈmɪnɪstə] *n.* 牧师

congregation [ˌkɒŋgrɪˈgeɪʃn] *n.* 教堂会众

constitute [ˈkɒnstɪtjuːt] *v.* 构成

gambling [ˈgæmblɪŋ] *n.* 赌博

merely [ˈmɪəlɪ] *adv.* 仅仅

commit [kəˈmɪt] *v.* 做；使……承担义务

charity [ˈtʃærɪtɪ] *n.* 施舍；慈善

contest [ˈkɒntest] *n.* 竞赛

# Raccoons

# 浣熊

## 爆笑故事

1 Part of my job at the state fish and wildlife department is to lend equipment to residents for trapping and relocating raccoons. A man who had been successful at capturing one of the animals called to ask whether raccoons mated for life. He said his daughter was worried that they might have separated a monogamous couple.

2 "I don't know why she's so concerned," he added. "She's been married three times."

## 点睛译文

1 我在州政府鱼类和野生动植物部门工作时，负责向居民们出借捕浣熊和重新安置浣熊的装备。一个人捕获了一只猎物，他打电话来询问浣熊是否终生只有一个伴侣。他说他的女儿担心他们可能拆散了一对终生伴侣。

2 他又补充说："我不知道她为什么这么关心这事，她自己已经结过3次婚了。"

## 生词宝库

wildlife [ˈwaɪldlaɪf] *n.* 野生动植物

department [dɪˈpɑːtmənt] *n.* 部；部门

equipment [ɪˈkwɪpmənt] *n.* 设备

resident [ˈrezɪdənt] *n.* 居民

raccoon [rəˈkuːn] *n.* 浣熊

capture [ˈkæptʃə] *v.* 捕获

monogamous [məˈnɒɡəməs] *adj.* 一夫一妻的

# Did You Know Him

# 你认识他吗

## 点睛译文

1 在朋友家的一次宴会上，主人提起一位高中时的校友。一位客人问他读书期间，某位副校长是否也在职。

2 “当然了，”主人答道，“他是我见过的最大的混蛋。你也认识他吗？”

3 “算是认识吧，”客人回答，“我妈妈上周六嫁给了他。”

## 爆笑故事

1 At a dinner party in the home of friends, our host mentioned his high school alma mater. One of the guests asked him if he had been a student there at the same time was a particular vice principal.

2 “I sure was!” answered the host. “He’s the biggest jerk I’ve ever met. Did you know him too?”

3 “Sort of,” replied the guest. “My mother married him last Saturday.”

## 生词宝库

mention [ˈmenʃn] *v.* 提起

alma mater [ˌælməˈmɑːtə] *n.* 母校

particular [pəˈtɪkjələ] *adj.* 特别的

principal [ˈprɪnsəpl] *n.* 校长

jerk [dʒɜːk] *n.* < 俚 > 蠢人

# A Mistake
# 搞错了

## 爆笑故事

1 An American, a Scot and a Canadian were killed in a car accident. They arrived at the gates of heaven, where a flustered St. Peter explained that there had been a mistake.

2 "Give me $500 each," he said, "and I'll return you to earth as if the whole thing never happened."

3 "Done!" said the American. Instantly, he found himself standing unhurt near the scene.

4 "Where are the others?" asked a medic.

5 "Last I knew," said the American, "the Scot was haggling price, and the Canadian was arguing that his government should pay."

## 点睛译文

1 一个美国人、一个苏格兰人和一个加拿大人在一场车祸中丧生。他们来到天堂的门口。在那里，醉醺醺的圣彼德解释说是搞错了。

2 "每人给我 500 美元，"他说，"我将把你们送回人间，就象什么都没有发生过一样。"

3 美国人说："成交！"马上，他发现自己毫不损伤地站在了现场附近。

4 一名医生问道："其他人在哪儿？"

5 那名美国人说："我离开之前，看见那个苏格兰人正在砍价，而那名加拿大人正在分辩说应该由他的政府来出这笔钱。"

## 生词宝库

accident [ˈæksɪdənt] *n.* 事故

arrive [əˈraɪv] *v.* 到达

gate [geɪt] *n.* 大门

fluster [ˈflʌstə] *v.* 使酩醉

instantly [ˈɪnstəntlɪ] *adv.* 立即地

haggle [ˈhægəl] *v.* 讨价还价

argue [ˈɑːgjuː] *v.* 争论

# Weather Predictions

# 天气预报

## 点睛译文

1 一个电影摄制组在沙漠深处工作。一天，一个印第安老人到导演跟前告诉导演说："明天下雨。"

2 第二天果然下雨了。

3 一周后，印第安人又来告诉导演说："明天有风暴。"

4 果然，第二天下了雹暴。

5 "印第安人真神，"导演说。他告诉秘书，雇佣该印第安人来预报天气。

6 几次预报都很成功。然后，接下来的两周，那个印第安老人一直没有出现。最后，导演派人去把他叫来了。

7 导演说："我明天必须得拍一个很大的场景，这得靠你了。明天天气如何啊？"

8 印第安人耸了耸肩。他说："我不知道，收音机坏了。"

## 爆笑故事

1 A film crew was on location deep in the desert. One day an old Indian went up to the director and said, "Tomorrow rain."

2 The next day it rained.

3 A week later, the Indian went up to the director and said, "Tomorrow storm."

4 The next day there was a hailstorm.

5 "This Indian is incredible," said the director. He told his secretary to hire the Indian to predict the weather.

6 However, after several successful predictions, the old Indian didn't show up for two weeks. Finally the director sent for him.

7 "I have to shoot a big scene tomorrow," said the director, "and I'm depending on you. What will the weather be like?"

8 The Indian shrugged his shoulders. "Don't know," he said. "Radio is broken."

## 生词宝库

crew [kruː] *n.*（一组）工作人员

location [ləʊˈkeɪʃən] *n.* 位置；地点；外景拍摄场地

desert [ˈdezət] *n.* 沙漠

hailstorm [ˈheɪlstɔːm] *n.* 雹暴

incredible [ɪnˈkredəbl] *adj.* 难以置信的

prediction [prɪˈdɪkʃn] *n.* 预言

shrug [ʃrʌg] *v.* 耸

# Roses for My Wife

# 给妻子的玫瑰

1 一天晚上回家的路上，我看到一家花店外面有一些刚剪下来的玫瑰。我挑了一打，走进店里，一个年轻的女售货员跟我打了个招呼。

2 她问道：“先生，这些是送给你妻子的吗？”

3 “是的。”我说。

4 “她的生日？”她问。

5 我回答：“不是。”

6 “你们的结婚纪念日？”

7 “不是。”我又答道。

8 当我将找回的钱装进口袋，朝门口走去时，那年轻的女人冲我喊道：“希望她能原谅你。”

## 爆笑故事

1 On the way home one night, I spotted some fresh-cut roses outside a florist's shop. After selecting a dozen and entering the shop, I was greeted by a young saleswoman.

2 “Are these for your wife, sir?” she asked.

3 “Yes,” I said.

4 “For her birthday?” she asked.

5 “No,” I replied.

6 “For your anniversary?”

7 “No,” I said again.

8 As I pocketed my change and headed toward the door, the young woman called out, “I hope she forgives you.”

## 生词宝库

spot [spɒt] *v.* < 口 > 看见

fresh-cut [f'reʃk'ʌt] *adj.* 刚剪下的

florist ['flɒrɪst] *n.* 花商

dozen ['dʌzn] *n.*（一）打；12 个

greet [gri:t] vt. 欢迎，迎接

anniversary [ænɪ'vɜ:sərɪ] *n.* 周年纪念日

pocket ['pɒkɪt] *v.* 装……在口袋里

forgive [fə'gɪv] *v.* 原谅

# Sleeping Pills
# 安眠药

## 爆笑故事

1 Bob was having trouble getting to sleep at night. He went to see his doctor, who prescribed some extra-strong sleeping pills.

2 Sunday night Bob took the pills, slept well and was awake before he heard the alarm. He took his time getting to the office, strolled in and said to his boss: "I didn't have a bit of trouble getting up this morning."

3 "That's fine," roared the boss, "but where were you Monday and Tuesday?"

## 点睛译文

1 鲍勃晚上失眠。他去看医生，医生给他开了一些强力安眠药。

2 星期天晚上鲍勃吃了药，睡得很好，早上在闹钟响之前就醒了过来。他到了办公室，遛达进去，对老板说："我今天早上起床一点都不费劲儿。"

3 "不错啊！" 老板吼道，"但是你星期一和星期二都去哪了？"

## 生词宝库

sleep [sliːp] *v.* 睡觉
prescribe [prɪˈskraɪb] *v.* 开处方
pill [pɪl] *n.* 药片
awake [əˈweɪk] *adj.* 醒着的
alarm [əˈlɑːm] *n.* 闹钟
stroll [strəʊl] *v.* 闲逛
roar [rɔː] *vi.* 咆哮

# Imitate Birds

# 模仿鸟儿

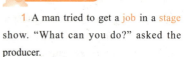

1 一个人想在一个舞台剧中找份工作。负责人问：“你能干什么呢？”

2 “模仿鸟儿。”那人说。

3 “你在开玩笑吧？”负责人答道，“那样的人一毛钱可以找一打。”

4 “噢，那就算了。”那名演员说着，然后就展开臂膀，飞出了窗口。

1 A man tried to get a job in a stage show. “What can you do?” asked the producer.

2 “Imitate birds.” the man said.

3 “Are you kidding?” answered the producer, “People like that are a dime a dozen.”

4 “Well, I guess that's that.” said the actor, as he spread his arms and flew out the window.

## 生词宝库

job [dʒɒb] *n.* 工作

stage [steɪdʒ] *n.* 舞台

imitate [ˈɪmɪteɪt] *v.* 模仿

kid [kɪd] *v.* 取笑

dime [daɪm] *n.* 一角硬币

spread [spred] *v.* 展开

# How Did You Ever Get Here 你是怎样来的

1 One winter morning, an employee explained why he had shown up for work 45 minutes late. "It was so slippery out that for every step I took ahead, I slipped back two."

2 The boss eyed him suspiciously. "Oh, yeah? Then how did you ever get here?"

3 "I finally gave up," he said, "and started for home."

1 一个冬天的早晨，一名员工解释他上班为什么迟到了 45 分钟 "外面太滑了，我每向前迈一步，就要向后退两步。"

2 老板狐疑地看着他。"噢，是吗？那你是怎样到这里来的？"

3 "后来我决定放弃，"他说，"然后我就往家里走。"

employee [ɪm'plɔɪiː] *n.* 雇员

show up 出现

slippery ['slɪpərɪ] *adj.* 滑的

suspiciously [sə'spɪʃəslɪ] *adv.* 猜疑地

# Creative
# 创造性

## 点睛译文

1 第一次求职时，我意识到在列举我所具备的为数不多的入职资格时，得有点创造性。当问及我是否接受过其它的培训时，我老实地回答说我花了 3 年时间学计算机程序设计课。我得到了那份工作。

2 我没有提到那门功课我重复学了 3 年才考及格。

## 爆笑故事

1 Applying for my first job, I realized I had to be creative in listing my few qualifications. Asked about additional schooling and training, I answered truthfully that I had spent three years in computer programming classes. I got the job.

2 I had neglected to mention that I took the same course for three years before I passed.

## 生词宝库

apply [ə'plaɪ] *v.* 申请

creative [kriː'eɪtɪv] *adj.* 有创造力的

list [lɪst] *v.* 列出

qualification [ˌkwɒlɪfɪ'keɪʃn] *n.* 资格

additional [ə'dɪʃənəl] *adj.* 附加的；额外的

truthfully ['truːθfəlɪ] *adv.* 说真话地

programming ['prəʊgræmɪŋ] *n.* 程序设计；[电脑]编程；

neglect [nɪ'glekt] *v.* 忽略

mention ['menʃən] vt. 提到

# CD Player
# CD唱机

## 爆笑故事

1 While shopping for my first CD player, I was able to decipher most of the technicals on the promotional signs. One designation had me puzzled, though, so I called over a salesperson and asked, "What does 'hybrid pulse D/A converter' mean?"

2 "That means," she said, "that this machine will read the digital information that is encoded on CDs and convert it into an audio signal — that is, into music."

3 "In other words, this CD player plays CDs."

4 "Exactly."

## 点睛译文

1 在购买我的第一部CD唱机时，我能够解读推销标记上面的大多数技术语言。但是有一个标示却让我颇为迷惑，于是我叫来销售商，问道："'混合脉冲D/A变换器'是什么意思？"

2 她说："它的意思是，这个机器能够读CD碟上加码的数字信息，再将它转换成声音信息——也就是说，转换成音乐。"

3 "换句话说，这个CD唱机能够播放CD碟。"

4 "正是如此。"

## 生词宝库

decipher [dɪ'saɪfə] *v.* 译解

promotional [prə'məʊʃənl] *adj.* 推销的

designation [ˌdezɪg'neɪʃn] *n.* 指示

puzzled ['pʌzld] *adj.* 困惑的

digital ['dɪdʒɪtl] *adj.* 数字的

convert [kən'vɜːt] *v.* 转变

signal ['sɪgnəl] *n.* 信号

# How Much Is It

# 多少钱

## 点睛译文

1 严冬来临，荷曼太太想采购一大批东西，所以她就一直等到周六丈夫有空的时候，拖着他去商店付钱顺便让他拎包裹。他们去了许多商店，荷曼太太买了一大堆东西。她经常停下脚步说：“看，乔！那个多漂亮！”

2 他总是回答：“好吧！亲爱的，多少钱？”然后掏钱去付款。

3 他们从最后一家商店出来的时候夜幕已经降临，荷曼先生已精疲力尽了。他心里想着其它事情，比如在家里暖暖的火炉边呷口美酒。突然，他太太仰望天空，说道：“看那月亮多美，乔！”

4 荷曼先生不加思索地答道：“好吧，亲爱的，多少钱？”

## 爆笑故事

1 It was winter, and Mrs. Hermann wanted to do a lot of shopping, so she waited until it was Saturday, when her husband was free, and she took him to the shops with her to pay for everything and to carry her parcels. They went to a lot of shops, and Mrs. Hermann bought a lot of things. She often stopped and said, “Look, Joe! Isn't that beautiful!”

2 He then answered, “All right, dear, How much is it?” and took his money out to pay for it.

3 It was dark when they came out of the last shop, and Mr. Hermann was tired and thinking about other things, like a nice drink by the side of a warm fire at home. Suddenly his wife looked up at the sky and said, “Look at that beautiful moon, Joe!”

4 Without stopping, Mr. Hermann answered, “All right, dear, How much is it?”

parcel [ˈpɑːsl] *n.* 包裹
answer [ˈɑːnsə] *v.* 回答
dark [dɑːk] *n.* 傍晚
warm [wɔːm] *adj.* 温暖的
fire [ˈfaɪə] *n.* 炉火
moon [muːn] *n.* 月亮

# Three Whistles
# 三声口哨

1 我答应过我的女朋友过生日送她一条金项链。可是当珠宝商报出我们看中的那条项链的价格时，我低低地打了个长口哨。

2 “那这条项链多少钱呢？”我指着另一个盘子里的项链问。

3 珠宝商答道：“先生，对你来说，大约值三声口哨。”

1 I promised my girlfriend a gold necklace for her birthday, but when the jeweler quoted a price for one we liked, I let out a long, low whistle.

2 “And how much are they then?” I asked, pointing to another tray.

3 “You, sir,” replied the jeweler, “about three whistles.”

## 生词宝库

promise [ˈprɒmɪs] *v.* 答应
necklace [ˈnekləs] *n.* 项链
jeweler [ˈdʒuːələ] *n.* 珠宝商
quote [kwəʊt] *v.* 开（价）
price [praɪs] *n.* 价格
whistle [ˈwɪsəl] *n.* 口哨

# Early Shopper
# 采购过早

1 It was Christmas and the judge was in a benevolent mood as he questioned the prisoner. "What are you charged with?" he asked.

2 "Doing my Christmas shopping early." replied the defendant.

3 "That's no offense." replied the judge, "How early were you doing this shopping?"

4 "Before the store opened." countered the prisoner.

## 点睛译文

1 那天是圣诞节，法官在审讯犯人时也有点恻隐之心。"你因为什么被起诉？"他问。

2 "采购圣诞节物品过早。"被告答。

3 法官回答："这不算犯法。你购物有多早？"

4 "在商店开门之前。"犯人应道。

## 生词宝库

benevolent [bə'nevələnt] *adj.* 仁慈的；乐善好施的

mood [mu:d] *n.* 情绪

charge [tʃɑ:dʒ] *v.* 控告

offense [ə'fens] *n.* 犯罪

counter ['kaʊntə] *v.* 反驳，回答

# Midway Tactics

# 中间战术

## 点睛译文

1 三个互相争生意的商店老板在一条商业街上租用了毗邻的店铺。旁观者们等着瞧好戏。

2 右边的零售商挂起了巨大的招牌，上书："大减价！""特便宜！"

3 左边的商店挂出了更大的招牌，声称："大砍价！""大折扣！"

4 中间的商店随后准备了一个大招牌，上面只简单地写着："入口处"。

## 爆笑故事

1 Three competing store owners rented adjoining shops in a mall. Observers waited for mayhem to ensue.

2 The retailer on the right put up huge signs saying, "Gigantic Sale!" and "Super Bargains!"

3 The store on the left raised bigger signs proclaiming, "Prices Slashed!" and "Fantastic Discounts!"

4 The owner in the middle then prepared a large sign that simply stated, "ENTRANCE".

## 生词宝库

competing [kəmˈpiːtɪŋ] *adj.* 竞争的

adjoining [əˈdʒɔɪnɪŋ] *adj.* 毗邻的

mayhem [ˈmeɪhem] *n.* 有意的破坏或暴行

retailer [ˈriːteɪlə] *n.* 零售商

gigantic [dʒaɪˈgæntɪk] *adj.* 巨大的

bargain [ˈbɑːgən] *n.* 便宜货

proclaim [prəˈkleɪm] *v.* 宣布

slash [slæʃ] *v.* 削减

fantastic [fænˈtæstɪk] *adj.* 不可思议的

discount [ˈdɪskaʊnt] *n.* 折扣

# The Cat's Doing the Pulling
# 是猫自己在拽

## 爆笑故事

1 Mother (reprimanding her small daughter): You mustn't pull the cat's tail.

2 Daughter: I'm only holding it, Mom. The cat's doing the pulling.

## 点睛译文

1 妈妈（正教训她的女儿）：你不该拽猫的尾巴。

2 女儿：妈妈，我只是握着猫尾巴，是它自己在拽。

## 生词宝库

small [smɔːl] *adj.* 幼小的，年幼的

pull [pʊl] *v.* 拉

tail [teɪl] *n.* 尾巴

hold [həʊld] *v.* 拿着

# I'm Glad
# 我很高兴

## 点睛译文

1 一个主日学校的老师正在对学生讲使别人高兴的重要性。

2 她说:“现在,孩子们,你们当中有谁让别人高兴过?”

3 “我,老师,”一个小男孩说,“昨天我就使别人高兴过。”

4 “做得好,是谁呢?”

5 “我奶奶。”

6 “好孩子,现在告诉我们,你是怎样使你奶奶高兴的。”

7 “是这样的,老师。我昨天去看她,在她那儿待了3个小时。然后我跟她说:‘奶奶,我要回家了。’她说:‘啊,我很高兴!’”

## 爆笑故事

1 A Sunday school teacher was telling her pupils the importance of making others glad.

2 “Now, children,” said she, “has anyone of you ever made someone else glad?”

3 “Please, teacher,” said a small boy, “I've made someone glad yesterday.”

4 “Well done. Who was that?”

5 “My granny.”

6 “Good boy. Now tell us how you made your grand mother glad.”

7 “Please, teacher, I went to see her yesterday, and stayed with her three hours. Then I said to her, ‘Granny, I'm going home,’ and she said, ‘Well, I'm glad’!”

## 生词宝库

pupil [ˈpjuːpl] *n.* 小学生

importance [ɪmˈpɔːtns] *n.* 重要

anyone [ˈenɪwʌn] *pron.* 任何人

glad [glæd] *adj.* 高兴的

# Birthday
# 生日

1 Professor: When is your birthday?

2 Kid: May 30.

3 Professor: Which year?

4 Kid: Every year.

点睛译文

1 教授：你的生日是什么时候？

2 孩子：5月30日。

3 教授：哪一年？

4 孩子：每年都是。

birthday [ˈbɜːθdeɪ] *n.* 生日

May [meɪ] *n.* 五月

# Does He Bite
# 它咬人吗

## 点睛译文

1 里基：我们又得到了一条新的狗，你愿意过来和他玩一会儿吗？

2 罗恩：嗯，我不知道——它咬人吗？

3 里基：这正是我想要知道的。

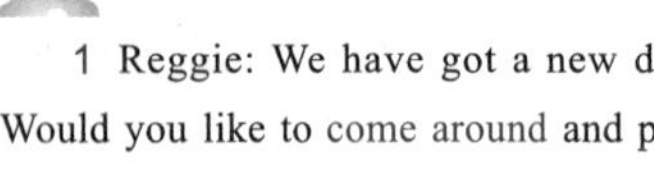

## 爆笑故事

1 Reggie: We have got a new dog. Would you like to come around and play with him?

2 Ron: Well, I don't know—does he bite?

3 Reggie: That's what I want to find out.

## 生词宝库

come around 顺便来访

bite [baɪt] *v.* 咬

find out 查明

# To Buy a Video
# 买录像机

## 爆笑故事

1 Amos asked his mother whether they could have a video.

2 "I'm afraid we can't afford one." sighed his mother.

3 But on the following day in came Amos, staggering beneath the weight of a brand-new video.

4 "How on earth did you pay for that?" gasped his mother.

5 "Easy, Mum." replied Amos, "I sold the television!"

## 点睛译文

1 阿莫斯问妈妈他们是否能买一台录像机。

2 "恐怕我们还买不起，"妈妈叹息着说。

3 可第二天，当艾莫斯回来时，他摇摇晃晃地搬着一台全新的录像机。

4 "你究竟是哪儿来的钱买这东西的？" 妈妈大吃一惊，喘着气说。

5 "妈妈，这简单，" 艾曼斯回答，"我把电视机给卖了。"

## 生词宝库

whether [ˈweðə] *conj.* 是否

video [ˈvɪdiəʊ] *n.* 录像机

afford [əˈfɔːd] *v.* 花费得起

sigh [saɪ] *v.* 叹息

stagger [ˈstægə] *v.* 摇摇晃晃

beneath [bɪˈniːθ] prep. 在……之下

gasp [gæsp] *v.* 喘着气说

television [ˈtelɪvɪʒən] *n.* 电视

# Boy, Oh Boy
# 让人无奈的孩子

## 点睛译文

1 我5岁的儿子和他的表弟在一起的时候，总要招来大乱。一个星期六，我开始抗议了。

2 “好啦，你们两个，”我严厉地说，“不许叫喊，不许乱拿，不许哭闹，不许乱敲，不许取笑，不许扯淡，不许弄坏玩具，不许乱抓，不许打架。”

3 我刚转身要走，就听我儿子说：“来，史蒂文，我们来把自己弄脏吧。”

## 爆笑故事

1 When they're together, my five-year-old son and his cousin tend to cause mayhem. One Saturday, I put my foot down.

2 "All right, you two," I said sternly. "No screaming, grabbing, whining, hitting, teasing, tattling, breaking toys, scratching or fighting."

3 As I turned to leave, I heard my son say, "C'mon, Steven, let's get dirty."

## 生词宝库

together [tə'geðə] *adv.* 共同；一起

cousin ['kʌzn] *n.* 堂（或表）兄弟（姐妹）

sternly [stɜːnlɪ] *adv.* 严厉地

grab [græb] *v.* 抓住；攫取

whine [waɪn] *v.* 哭闹；抱怨

tease [tiːz] *v.* 取笑

tattle ['tætəl] *v.* 闲谈

scratch [skrætʃ] *v.* 抓

# Reason of Punishment
# 惩罚的原因

1 One day a little girl came home from school, and said to her mother, "Mommy, today in school I was punished for something that I didn't do."

2 The mother exclaimed, "But that's terrible! I'm going to have a talk with your teacher about this! By the way, what was it that you didn't do?"

3 The little girl replied, "My homework."

点睛译文

1 一天，小女孩从学校回到家里，对妈妈说："妈妈，今天在学校里我因为一件没有做过的事情而受到了惩罚。"

2 妈妈激动地说："那真是太可怕了！我要跟你的老师好好谈一谈。对了，你没有做过的那件事是什么？"

3 小女孩回答说："我的家庭作业。"

生词宝库

punish [ˈpʌnɪʃ] *v.* 惩罚

exclaim [ɪkˈskleɪm] *v.* 大叫

terrible [ˈterəbl] *adj.* 可怕的

homework [ˈhəʊmwɜːk] *n.* 家庭作业

# Reason For Being Late

# 迟到的原因

1 迈克上学迟到了。他对布莱克老师说："对不起，老师，今天早上我迟到了。因为我在梦里观看了一场球赛。"

2 "为什么这会让你迟到呢？"老师问道。

3 迈克回答说："因为这两个队都没有能力获胜，所以就持续了很长时间。"

1 Mike was late for school. He said to his teacher, Mr. Black, "Excuse me for my coming late, sir. I watched a football match in my dream."

2 "Why did it make you late?" inquired the teacher.

3 "Because neither team could win the game, so it lasted a long time." replied Mike.

## 生词宝库

football [ˈfʊtbɔːl] *n.* <英>足球；<美>橄榄球

match [mætʃ] *n.* 比赛

inquire [ɪnˈkwaɪə] *v.* 询问

team [tiːm] *n.* 队

# But the Teacher Cried
# 可是老师哭了

## 爆笑故事

1 The six-year-old John was terribly spoiled. His father knew it, but his grandma doted on him. He hardly left her side. And when he wanted anything, he either cried or threw a temper tantrum. Then came his first day of school, his first day away from his grandmother's loving arms.

2 When he came home from school his grandma met him at the door. "Was school all right?" she asked, "Did you get along all right? Did you cry?"

3 "Cry?" John asked. "No, I didn't cry, but the teacher did!"

## 点睛译文

1 6岁的约翰娇生惯养。他的父亲知道这一点，可他的祖父母仍然宠着他。这孩子几乎寸步不离他的祖母。他想要什么，不是哭，就是闹。他第一天上学才离开祖母的怀抱。

2 约翰放学了，他奶奶在门口接他并问道："学校怎么样？你过得好吗？哭了没有？"

3 "哭？"约翰问，"不，我没哭，可老师哭了。"

## 生词宝库

terribly [ˈterəblɪ] *adv.* <口> 非常地；很

spoil [spɔɪl] *v.* 宠坏

dote [dəʊt] *v.* 溺爱

temper [ˈtempə] *n.* 脾气

tantrum [ˈtæntrəm] *n.* 发脾气

# Two Birds

# 两只鸟

1 Teacher: Here are two birds — one is a swallow, the other is sparrow. Now who can tell us which is which?

2 Student: I cannot point out but I know the answer.

3 Teacher: Please tell us.

4 Student: The swallow is beside the sparrow and the sparrow is beside the swallow.

## 点睛译文

1 老师：这儿有两只鸟，一只是燕子一只是麻雀。谁能指出哪只是燕子，哪只是麻雀？

2 学生：我指不出，但我知道答案。

3 老师：请说说看。

4 学生：燕子旁边的就是麻雀，麻雀旁边的就是燕子。

swallow [ˈswɒləʊ] *n.* 燕子

sparrow [ˈspærəʊ] *n.* 麻雀

point out 指出

beside [bɪˈsaɪd] *prep.* 在……旁边

# A Present
# 凯特的礼物

1 Kate: Mom, do you know what I'm going to give you for your birthday?

2 Mom: No, honey, what?

3 Kate: A nice teapot.

4 Mom: But I've got a nice teapot.

5 Kate: No, you haven't. I've just dropped it.

## 点睛译文

1 凯特：妈妈，你知道我要给你一件什么生日礼物吗？

2 妈妈：不知道，宝贝，是什么呀？

3 凯特：一个漂亮的茶壶。

4 妈妈：可是我已经有一个漂亮的茶壶了呀。

5 凯特：不，你没有了。我刚刚把它给摔了。

## 生词宝库

honey [ˈhʌnɪ] *n.* 宝贝

nice [naɪs] *adj.* 吸引人的

teapot [ˈtiːpɒt] *n.* 茶壶

drop [drɒp] *v.*（使）落下

# A Nail or a Fly
# 钉子还是苍蝇

## 点睛译文

1 一位视力正在衰退的老绅士住进了一家旅馆的客房。他双手各拿了一瓶酒。在墙上有只苍蝇，他误以为是枚钉子。他把两只瓶子朝上一挂，瓶子掉下来摔碎了，酒洒了一地。

2 一个女服务员知道事情的来龙去脉以后，对他深表同情，决定帮他个忙。

3 于是，第二天早上他到楼顶花园散步时，她把一枚钉子钉在了苍蝇停过的地方。

4 这次，老人回到了房里。弥漫的酒味让他想起了那件事。他抬头往墙上一看，苍蝇又停在了那儿！他轻手轻脚地走近，使尽全力拍了一掌。

5 听到一声大叫，好心的女服务员冲进房来。让她大

## 爆笑故事

1 An old gentleman whose eyesight was failing came to stay in a hotel room with a bottle of wine in each hand. On the wall there was a fly which he took for a nail. So the moment he hung them on, the bottles fell broken and the wine spilt all over the floor.

2 When a waitress discovered what had happened, she showed deep sympathy for him and decided to do him a favor.

3 So the next morning when he was out taking a walk in the roof garden, she hammered a nail exactly where the fly had stayed.

4 Now the old man entered his room. The smell of the spilt wine reminded him of the accident. When he looked up at the wall, he found the fly was there again! He walked to it carefully and slapped it with all his strength.

5 On hearing a loud cry, the kind-hearted waitress rushed in. To her great

surprise, the poor old man was there sitting on the floor, his teeth clenched and his right hand bleeding!

为吃惊的是，可怜的老头正坐在地板上，牙关紧咬，右手滴血不止。

eyesight [ˈaɪsaɪt] *n.* 视力
nail [neɪl] *n.* 钉子
spill [spɪl] *v.* 溢出
sympathy [ˈsɪmpəθɪ] *n.* 同情
roof [ruːf] *n.* 屋顶
clench [klentʃ] *v.* 紧咬
bleed [bliːd] *v.* 流血

# Sharing the Apples

# 分苹果

1 妈妈给了哈里两个苹果，一个大一点，另一个小点儿。

2 “跟妹妹分着吃。”妈妈说。

3 所以，哈里就把小个的给了妹妹，自己开始啃那个大个的。

4 “哼！” 妹妹说，“如果妈妈给了我，我会把大的给你，把小的留给自己的。”

5 “对呀，”哈里说，“你拿到的不就是小的吗，那还着个什么急呀？”

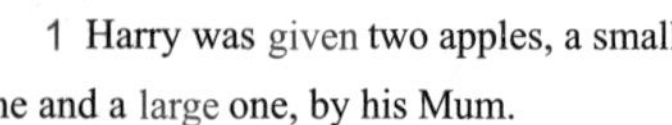


1 Harry was given two apples, a small one and a large one, by his Mum.

2 “Share them with your sister.” she said.

3 So Harry gave the small one to his little sister and started touching into the large one.

4 “Cor!” said his sister, “If Mum had given them to me I’d have given you the large one and had the small one myself.”

5 “Well,” said Harry, “that’s what you’ve got, so what are you worrying about?”

生词宝库

give [gɪv] *v.* 给

large [lɑːdʒ] *adj.* 大的

share [ʃeə] *v.*（平均）分享，共享

touch [tʌtʃ] *v.* 吃

worry [ˈwʌrɪ] *v.* 担心

# Intelligent Son
# 聪明的儿子

1 One day, the father let his eight year-old son send a letter. The son took the letter; the father then remembered he didn't write the address and addressee's name on the envelope.

2 After the son came back, the father asked him: "You have thrown the letter in the mail box?"

3 "Certainly."

4 "You have not seen there is no address or the addressee name on the envelope?"

5 "I certainly saw nothing written on the envelope."

6 "Then why you didn't take it back?"

7 "I also thought that you did not write the address and the addressee because you did not want me to know whom you send the letter to!"

点睛译文

1 有一天，父亲让8岁的儿子去寄一封信，儿子已经拿着信跑了，父亲才想起信封上没写地址和收信人的名字。

2 儿子回来后，父亲问他："你把信丢进邮筒了吗？"

3 "当然。"

4 "你没看见信封上没有写地址和收信人的名字吗？"

5 "我当然看见信封上什么也没写"

6 "那你为什么不拿回来呢？"

7 "我还以为你不写地址和收信人，是为了不想让我知道你把信寄给谁呢！"

生词宝库

letter [ˈletə] *n.* 信
remember [rɪˈmembə] *v.* 想起
address [əˈdres] *n.* 地址
envelope [ˈenvələup] *n.* 信封
mail box [meil bɔks] *n.* 信箱

# Snorer
# 瞌睡者

## 点睛译文

1 牧师非常生气，因为总有一个人在他说教时打瞌睡。

2 一个星期天，正当坐在前排的那个人又在瞌睡时，牧师决定要好好教育他一下，让他不要再在布道时睡觉。于是他低声对信徒们说：

3 “想去天堂的人，都请站起来吧。”

4 所有的人都站了起来——除了那个打瞌睡的人。在低声说过请坐后，牧师高声喊道：“想去下地狱的人请站起来！”

5 打瞌睡的人被这突然的喊叫声惊醒了，他站了起来。看到牧师高站在教坛上，正生气地看着他。

6 这个人说道：“噢，先生，我不知道我们在选什么，但看上去只有你和我是候选人。”

## 爆笑故事

1 The preacher was vexed because a certain member of his congregation always fell asleep during the sermon.

2 As the man was snoring in the front row one Sunday, the preacher determined he would teach him not to sleep during the sermon. So, in a whisper, he asked the congregation.

3 “All who want to go to Heaven please rise.”

4 Everyone got up except the snorer. After whispering “Be seated”, the minister shouted at the top of his voiced, “All those who want to be with the devil, please rise.”

5 Awaking with a start, the sleepy-head jumped to his feet and saw the preacher standing tall and angry in the pulpit.

6 “Well, sir.” he said, “I don't know what we're voting on, but it looks like you and me are the only ones for it.”

生词宝库

preacher [ˈpriːtʃə] *n.* 牧师

congregation [ˌkɒŋgrɪˈgeɪʃn] *n.* 教堂会众

snore [snɔː] *v.* 打鼾

whisper [ˈwɪspə] *v.* 低声说

devil [ˈdevəl] *n.* 魔鬼

pulpit [ˈpʊlpɪt] *n.* 讲道坛

# Stupid Question
# 愚蠢的问题

## 点睛译文

1 丹在一个大城市的某个俱乐部当守门人。每天都有数千人经过他的门口，而且许多人都会停下来问他："请问现在几点？"

2 几个月后，丹想："我不想再回答这些蠢人提出的问题了，我要去买一只大钟，把它挂在这儿的墙上。"于是他买了一只钟，把它挂在了墙上。

3 "现在人们总不会再停下来问我时间了吧。"他高兴地想。

4 可是打那以后，每天仍有许多人停下来，看看钟，然后问丹："这钟准吗？"

## 爆笑故事

1 Dan was the doorman of a club in a big city. Everyday, thousands of people passed his door, and a lot of them stopped and asked him, "What's the time, please?"

2 After a few months, Dan said to himself, "I'm not going to answer all those stupid people any more. I'm going to buy a big clock and put it upon the wall here." Then he did so.

3 "Now people aren't going to stop and ask me the time." he thought happily.

4 But after that, a lot of people stopped, looked at the clock and then asked Dan, "Is that clock right?"

## 生词宝库

doorman [ˈdɔːmən] *n.* 看门人

pass [pɑːs] *v.* 经过

stupid [ˈstjuːpɪd] *adj.* 愚蠢的

stop [stɒp] *v.* 停下

# Put Your Feet In

# 把脚放进去

## 爆笑故事

1 The school girl was sitting with her feet stretched far out into the aisle, and was busily chewing gum, when the teacher espied her.

2 "Mary!" called the teacher sharply.

3 "Yes, Madam?" questioned the pupil.

4 "Take that gum out of your mouth and put your feet in!"

## 点睛译文

1 一个女学生坐在座位上，嘴里起劲地嚼着口香糖，脚却伸到课桌间的走道里，被老师发现了。

2 "玛丽！"老师严厉地叫她。

3 "什么事，老师？"这女学生问。

4 "把口香糖从嘴里拿出来，把脚放进去！"

## 生词宝库

stretch [stretʃ] *v.* 伸展
chew [tʃuː] *v.* 咀嚼
gum [gʌm] *n.* 口香糖
espy [eˈspaɪ] *v.* 看到；发现
sharply [ˈʃɑːplɪ] *adv.* 严厉地

# Five Months Older

# 大5个月

1 第二次世界大战开始了，约翰想参军，可他只有16岁，当时规定男孩到18岁才能入伍。所以军医给他进行体检时，他说他已经18岁了。

2 可约翰的哥哥刚入伍没几天，而且也是这个军医给他做的检查。这位医生还记得他哥哥的姓。所以当他看到约翰的表格时，感到非常惊奇。

3 “你多大了？”军医问。

4 “18，长官。”约翰说。

5 “可你的哥哥也是18岁，你们是双胞胎吗？”

6 约翰脸红了，说：“哦，不是，长官，我哥哥比我大5个月。”

1 The Second World War had begun, and John wanted to join the army, but he was only 16 years old, and boys were allowed to join only if they were over 18. So when the army doctor examined him, he said that he was 18.

2 But John's brother had joined the army a few days before, and the same doctor had examined him too. This doctor remembered the older boy's family name, so when he saw John's papers, he was surprised.

3 "How old are you?" he said.

4 "Eighteen, sir." said John.

5 "But your brother was eighteen, too." said the doctor. "Are you twins?"

6 "Oh, no, sir." said John, and his face went red. "My brother is five months older than I am."

## 生词宝库

army [ˈɑːmɪ] *n.* 军队

allow [əˈlaʊ] *v.* 允许

examine [ɪɡˈzæmɪn] *v.* 检查

surprised [səˈpraɪzd] *adj.* 惊讶的

# Give up Your Seat to a Lady
# 给女士让座

1 Little Johnny says, "Mom, when I was on the bus with Daddy this morning, he told me to give up my seat to a lady."

2 "You've done the right thing." says Mommy.

3 "But Mommy, I was sitting on daddy's lap."

**点睛译文**

1 小强尼说："妈妈，今天早上和爸爸在公交车上时，他叫我给一位女士让座。"

2 妈妈说："你做得很对呀。"

3 "但是，妈妈，我是坐在爸爸膝盖上的。"

**生词宝库**

lady [ˈleɪdɪ] *n.* 女士

right [raɪt] *adj.* 正确的

lap [læp] *n.* 膝部

# Jump Up and Down

# 跳上跳下

**点睛译文**

1 妈妈：你为什么不停地跳上跳下的？

2 汤姆：我刚吃完药，可我忘了喝前先摇摇瓶子。

**爆笑故事**

1 Mother: Why are you jumping up and down?

2 Tom: I've just taken some medicine and I forgot to shake the bottle.

**生词宝库**

medicine [ˈmedsɪn] *n.* 药

shake [ʃeɪk] *v.* 摇动

# The Cigarettes Will Be on Fire 烟卷迟早都会点着

1 Mary was so disgusted at her husband's cigarette smoking that she complained to him one day.

2 "I hope that all the cigarette factories will catch fire someday."

3 "Don't worry, dear. All the cigarettes will be on fire sooner or later." He said with a smile.

## 点睛译文

1 玛丽非常讨厌丈夫吸烟，一天她对他抱怨说：

2 "我希望有一天所有的卷烟厂都失火。"

3 "不用担心，亲爱的，所有的烟卷迟早都会点着的。"他笑着说。

disgusted [dɪsˈɡʌstɪd] *adj.* 厌恶的

husband [ˈhʌzbənd] *n.* 丈夫

cigarette [sɪɡəˈret] *n.* 香烟

complain [kəmˈpleɪn] *v.* 抱怨

factory [ˈfæktrɪ] *n.* 工厂

# I Understand Him
# 我懂他的话

## 点睛译文

1 在饭店吃饭的时候，我斥责我 4 岁的儿子满嘴含着食物跟人说话。

2 “喔，呢。”我听到的就是这些。

3 “德鲁，”我责备道，“没人明白你在说什么。”

4 我丈夫平静地说：“他说他要一些番茄酱。”

5 坐在旁边的一位妇女靠过来问道：“你究竟是如何明白他的话的呢？”

6 “我是牙医。”我丈夫解释道。

## 爆笑故事

1 While eating in a restaurant, I reprimanded my four-year-old son for speaking with his mouth full.

2 “Mump umn Kmpfhm,” was all I heard.

3 “Drew,” I scolded, “no one can understand a word you’re saying.”

4 “He says he wants some ketchup.” my husband said calmly.

5 A woman sitting nearby leaned over and asked, “How in the world did you understand him?”

6 “I’m a dentist.” my husband explained.

## 生词宝库

nearby [ˌnɪəˈbaɪ] *adv.* 在附近

lean [liːn] *v.* 斜靠

dentist [ˈdentɪst] *n.* 牙科医生

# I've Come to Install the Phone 我是来装电话的

## 爆笑故事

1 A young businessman had just started his business, and rented a beautiful office. Sitting there, he saw a man come into the outer office. Wishing to appear busy, the businessman picked up the phone and pretended that he had a big deal working. He threw huge figures around and made giant commitments.

2 Finally, he hung up and asked the visitor. "Can I help you?"

3 The man said: "Sure. I've come to install the phone."

## 点睛译文

1 一个年轻人刚刚开始做生意，就租了一个漂亮的办公室。一天，他坐在办公室里，看到有一个人在外面，于是他就装作生意很忙的样子，拿起电话胡吹乱侃，还不停地甩出几个大数字，好像在谈一笔大买卖一样。

2 到了最后，他终于挂了电话，问来访的人："有事儿吗？"

3 那个人回答："是啊，我是来给你安装电话的。"

## 生词宝库

businessman [ˈbɪznəsmæn] *n.* 商人

outer [ˈaʊtə] *adj.* 外部的

figure [ˈfɪgə] *n.* 数字

commitment [kəˈmɪtmənt] *n.* 承诺，保证

install [ɪnˈstɔl] *v.* 安装

# A Neuropathy
# 一个神经病

1 有一个神经病，不知道从哪里弄来了一把手枪。有一天他走在一条小黑胡同里，突然遇上一个年轻人，神经病二话不说将其按在地上用枪指着他的头。问道，“一加一得几。”

2 年轻人吓坏了，沉思了很久。回答：“等于二。”

3 神经病毫不犹豫的打死了他。然后把抢揣在怀里，冷冷地说了一句：“你知道的太多了……”

1 There is a neuropathy. No one knows how he has got a pistol. One day he was walking in a small black alley. When suddenly a young man showed, the neuropathy said nothing but to held him on the ground and point his pistol at his head, asks, “What is one plus one?”

2 Terrified as the young people, he thought for a long time and answered, “Two.”

3 The neuropathy then killed him without hesitation. And then he held the pistol in his arms and said in a cold voice, “You’ve known too much ...”

**生词宝库**

neuropathy [ˌnjʊəˈrɒpəθɪ] *n.* 神经病
pistol [ˈpɪstl] *n.* 手枪
alley [ˈælɪ] *n.* 胡同
plus [plʌs] prep. 加
terrified [ˈterɪfaɪd] *adj.* 受惊吓的
hesitation [hezɪˈteɪʃn] *n.* 犹豫

# Drunk
# 醉酒

## 爆笑故事

1 One day, a father and his little son were going home. At this age, the boy was interested in all kinds of things and was always asking questions.

2 Now, he asked: "What's the meaning of the word 'Drunk', dad?"

3 "Well, my son," his father replied, "look, there are standing two policemen. If I regard the two policemen as four then I am drunk."

4 "But, dad," the boy said, "there's only one policeman!"

## 点睛译文

1 一天，父亲与小儿子一道回家。这个孩子正处于那种对什么事都很感兴趣的年龄，老是有提不完的问题。

2 他向父亲发问道："爸爸，'醉'字是什么意思？"

3 父亲回答说："唔，孩子，你瞧那儿站着两个警察。如果我把他们看成了四个，那么我就算醉了。"

4 "可是，爸爸，"孩子说，"那儿只有一个警察呀！"

## 生词宝库

age [eɪdʒ] *n.* 年龄
interested [ˈɪntrəstɪd] *adj.* 感兴趣的
question [ˈkwestʃən] *n.* 问题
meaning [ˈmiːnɪŋ] *n.* 意义
drunk [drʌŋk] *adj.* 喝醉了的
regard [rɪˈgɑːd] *v.* 把……看做

# Hospitality
# 好客

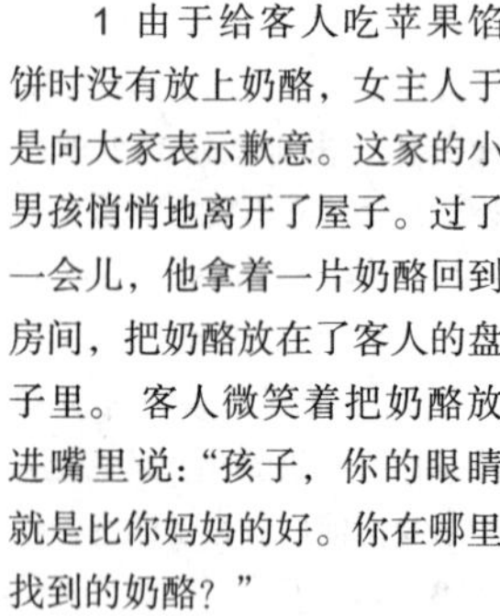

1 由于给客人吃苹果馅饼时没有放上奶酪，女主人于是向大家表示歉意。这家的小男孩悄悄地离开了屋子。过了一会儿，他拿着一片奶酪回到房间，把奶酪放在了客人的盘子里。 客人微笑着把奶酪放进嘴里说：“孩子，你的眼睛就是比你妈妈的好。你在哪里找到的奶酪？”

2 “在捕鼠夹上，先生。”那小男孩说。

1 The hostess apologized to her unexpected guest for serving an apple-pie without any cheese. The little boy of the family left the room quietly for a moment and returned with a piece of cheese which he laid on the guest's plate. The visitor smiled, put the cheese into his mouth and then said, “You must have better eyes than your mother, sonny. Where did you find the cheese?”

2 “In the rat-trap, sir.” replied the boy.

## 生词宝库

hostess [ˈhəʊstəs] *n.* 女主人
apologize [əˈpɒlədʒaɪz] *v.* 道歉
quietly [ˈkwaɪətlɪ] *adv.* 安静地
cheese [tʃiːz] *n.* 奶酪
sonny [ˈsʌnɪ] *n.* 小家伙；宝贝（口语昵称）
rat [ræt] *n.* 鼠

# Things Have Been Okay

# 一切都正常

## 爆笑故事

1 A young couple was becoming anxious about their four-year-old son, who had not yet talked. They took him to specialists, but the doctors found nothing wrong with him. Then one morning at breakfast the boy suddenly blurted, "Mom, the toast is burned."

2 "You talked! You talked!" Shouted his mother. "I'm so happy! But why has it taken this long?"

3 "Well, up till now," said the boy, "things have been okay."

## 点睛译文

1 一对年轻夫妇有个儿子，已经4岁了，还没有开口说话，他们对此深感焦虑。他们带他去找专家诊治，但医生们总觉得他没有毛病。后来有一天早上吃早餐时，那孩子突然开口了："妈妈，面包烤焦了。"

2 "你说话了！你说话了！"他母亲叫了起来。"我太高兴了！但为什么花了这么长的时间你才说话呢？"

3 那男孩说，"哦，在这之前，一切都很正常。"

## 生词宝库

couple [ˈkʌpl] *n.*（一）对
anxious [ˈæŋkʃəs] *adj.* 焦急的
specialist [ˈspeʃəlɪst] *n.* 专家
breakfast [ˈbrekfəst] *n.* 早餐
blurt [blɜːt] *v.* 冲口说出
toast [təʊst] *n.* 烤面包

# Akimbo
# 叉腰

1 像大多数别的小孩一样，两岁的伊米莉亚不爱洗手，每次弄脏手，随便在身上一抹就得了。

2 一天我正陪她吃炸知了，她手上的油多了，便习惯地往真丝小褂子上蹭，我阻止道：“你想干什么？”

3 她马上意识到问题所在，从容答道：“我叉腰。”

## 爆笑故事

1 Just like most of other kids, aged two Emilia didn't like washing hands—she's always wiping the dirt off hands on her clothes.

2 One day I accompanied her to have fried cicadae. Habitually she rubbed her grease fingers on her real silk short gown. I held back her from doing it: “What do you want to do?”

3 She was immediately on to her blame, replied at ease: “I'm akimbo.”

## 生词宝库

kid [kɪd] *n.* 小孩
wipe [waɪp] *v.* 擦
dirt [dɜːt] *n.* 污垢
accompany [əˈkʌmpənɪ] *v.* 陪伴
cicada [sɪˈkɑːdə] *n.* 蝉
grease [griːs] *n.* 油脂
silk [sɪlk] *n.* 丝绸
blame [bleɪm] *n.* 过失，过错

# I'm the Only Driver
# 唯有我是司机

## 爆笑故事

1 A short young man was running behind a bus which was full of passengers. But the bus still ran at a great speed.

2 "Stop, stop." a passenger looked out of the window, and shouted at the young man, "You can't catch it!"

3 "I must." the young fellow said, out of breath, "Because I'm the only driver of the bus."

## 点睛译文

1 在一辆满载乘客的公共汽车后面，一位小个子青年在奔跑着。汽车仍在高速前进。

2 "停下吧，停下吧。"一位乘客把头伸出窗子，对小个子喊道，"你追不上的！"

3 "我必须追上。"小个子气喘吁吁地说，"只有我是这辆车的司机！"

## 生词宝库

passenger [ˈpæsɪndʒə] *n.* 乘客

speed [spiːd] *n.* 速度

window [ˈwɪndəʊ] *n.* 窗户

fellow [ˈfeləʊ] *n.* 家伙，小伙子

# Employer and Employee
# 雇主和雇员

## 点睛译文

1 工人：布朗先生，我想请您给我加一点工资。我刚刚结了婚。

2 雇主：非常抱歉，老兄，我无能为力。对工人在厂外发生的事故我们概不负责。

## 爆笑故事

1 Workman: Mr. Brown, I should like to ask for a small rise in my wages. I have just been married.

2 Employer: Very sorry, my dear man, but I can't help you. For accidents which happen to our workmen outside the factory we are not responsible.

## 生词宝库

workman [ˈwɜːkmən] *n.* 工人

rise [raɪz] *n.* 上升

wage [weɪdʒ] *n.* 工资

responsible [rɪˈspɒnsəbl] *adj.* 有责任的

# The New Teacher
# 新老师

1 George comes from school on the first of September.

2 "George, how did you like your new teacher?" asked his mother.

3 "I didn't like her, Mother, because she said that three and three were six and then she said that two and four were six too…"

点睛译文

1 9月1日，乔治放学回到家里。

2 "乔治，你喜欢你们的新老师吗？"妈妈问。

3 "妈妈，我不喜欢，因为她说3加3得6，可后来又说2加4也得6……"

September [sepˈtembə] *n.* 九月

new [njuː] *adj.* 新的

# An Absent Minded Professor 心不在焉的教授

1 有一天，人们看见一个教授在路上走，他心不在焉的特点已是众所周知。只见他的一只脚一直踏在街沟里，另一只脚踩在人行道上。

2 他的一个学生碰见他，说："晚上好，教授，您好吗？"

3 "哦。"这个教授回答说，"我想着，离开家时我还挺好的，可是现在也不知道是怎么了，我已经一瘸一拐走了半个小时了。"

爆笑故事

1 A notoriously absent minded professor was one day observed walking along the street with one foot continually in the gutter, the other on the pavement.

2 A pupil meeting him said: "Good evening, professor. How are you?"

3 "Well." answered the professor, "I thought I was all right when I left home, but now I don't know what's the matter with me, I've been limping for the last half hour."

生词宝库

absent minded [ˈæbsəntˈmaɪndɪd] *adj.* 心不在焉的

observe [əbˈzɜːv] *v.* 看到

continually [kənˈtɪnjʊəlɪ] *adv.* 不断地

gutter [ˈgʌtə] *n.* 街边水沟

pavement [ˈpeɪvmənt] *n.* 人行道

limp [lɪmp] *v.* 跛行

# It's His Fault
# 他的错

1 Billy and Bobby were small boys. They were brothers and they often had fights with each other.

2 Last Saturday their mother said to them, "I'm going to cook our lunch now. Go out and play in the garden — and be good."

3 "Yes, Mummy." the two boys answered and they went out. They played in the garden for half an hour, and then Billy ran into the kitchen.

4 "Mummy," he said, "Bobby's broken a window in Mrs. Allen's house."

5 Mrs. Allen was one of their neighbors.

6 "He's a bad boy," his mother said. "How did he break it?"

7 "I threw a stone at him," Billy answered, "and he quickly moved down."

## 点睛译文

1 比利和博比都是小男孩，他们是兄弟，两人经常打架。

2 上个星期六，他们的妈妈对他们说："我现在要做午饭了。去，到花园去玩吧，别淘气。"

3 "好的，妈妈。" 两个男孩回答，然后他们就出去了。他们在花园里玩了半个小时，然后比利跑进了厨房。

4 "妈妈，" 他说，"博比打碎了艾伦太太家的窗玻璃。"

5 艾伦太太是他们的邻居。

6 "他是个坏孩子，" 他的妈妈说，"他是怎么把玻璃打碎的？"

7 "我朝他扔了一块石子，" 比利回答，"但他快速地蹲下了。"

## 生词宝库

fight [faɪt] *n.* 打架

Saturday [ˈsætədeɪ] *n.* 星期六

cook [kʊk] *v.* 烹调

lunch [lʌntʃ] *n.* 午餐

neighbor [ˈneɪbə] *n.* 邻居

# Three Pastors

# 三个牧师

1 三个南部的牧师在一家小餐馆里吃午饭。其中的一个说道：“你们知道吗，自从夏天来临，我教堂的阁楼和顶楼就被蝙蝠骚扰，我用尽了一切办法——噪音、喷雾、猫——似乎什么都不能把它们赶走。”

2 另外一位说：“是啊，我也有同种困扰。在我的钟楼和阁楼也有好几百只。我曾经请人把整个地方用烟熏消毒一遍，它们还是赶不走。”

3 第三个牧师说：“我为我那里的所有蝙蝠洗礼，让它们成为教会的一员……从此一只也没有再回来过。”

## 爆笑故事

1 Three pastors in the south were having lunch in a diner. One said, “You know, since summer started I've been having trouble with bats in my loft and attic at church. I've tried everything — noise, spray, cats — nothing seems to scare them away.”

2 Another said, “Yes, me too. I've got hundreds living in my belfry and in the attic. I've been had the place fumigated, and they still won't go away.”

3 The third said, “I baptized all mine, and made them members of the church... haven't seen one back since!”

## 生词宝库

pastor [ˈpɑːstə] *n.* 牧师

diner [ˈdaɪnə] *n.* 小餐馆

loft [lɒft] *n.* 阁楼

attic [ˈætɪk] *n.* 顶楼

spray [spreɪ] *n.* 喷雾

scare [skeə] *v.* 吓走

fumigate [ˈfjuːmɪgeɪt] *v.* 熏制

baptize [bæpˈtaɪz] *v.* 给……施浸礼；洗礼

# The Ability of the Kangaroo 袋鼠的能力

## 爆笑故事

1 The zoo built a special eight-foot-high enclosure for its newly acquired kangaroo, but the next morning the animal was found hopping around outside.

2 The height of the fence was increased to 15 feet, but the kangaroo got out again. Exasperated, the zoo director had the height increased to 30 feet, but the kangaroo still escaped.

3 A giraffe asked the kangaroo, "How high do you think they'll build the fence?"

4 "I don't know," said the kangaroo, "Maybe a thousand feet if they keep leaving the gate unlocked."

## 点睛译文

1 动物园为刚引进的袋鼠建了一个特殊的8英尺高的围墙。但是第二天早上，人们发现这动物在围墙外面蹦蹦跳跳。

2 于是围墙高度增加到15英尺，但袋鼠还是跑了出来。动物园经理甚感恼火，又叫人把围墙高度加到30英尺，但袋鼠还是逃了出来。

3 长颈鹿问袋鼠："你认为他们会把围墙建到多高？"

4 "我不知道，"袋鼠说，"如果他们继续开着大门，可能要修到1000英尺吧。"

## 生词宝库

enclosure [ɪnˈkləʊʒə] *n.* 围墙
kangaroo [ˌkæŋgəˈruː] *n.* 袋鼠
height [haɪt] *n.* 高度
fence [fens] *n.* 栅栏
exasperated [ɪgˈzæspəreɪtɪd] *adj.* 恼火的
director [dɪˈrektə] *n.* 经理
increase [ɪnˈkriːs] *v.* 增加
giraffe [dʒəˈrɑːf] *n.* 长颈鹿

# It Has a Lifetime Warranty
# 终身保修

1 在将母亲下葬9个月后，当地殡仪馆的一个客户终于攒够了钱去买那副他早就相中的价值不菲的棺材了。他把母亲的棺材挖了出来，将尸体转移到了那副新的钢制棺材中。

2 “这副棺材有什么特别？”我问葬礼的承办人。

3 他回答说：“这种棺材终生保修。”

1 After burying his mother nine months earlier, a client of the local mortuary finally had enough money to purchase the expensive coffin he'd originally wanted. So he exhumed the body and transferred his deceased mother into the new steel casket.

2 “What's so special about this coffin?” I asked the funeral director.

3 He replied: “It has a lifetime warranty.”

## 生词宝库

bury [ˈberɪ] *v.* 埋葬
client [ˈklaɪənt] *n.* 客户，委托人
mortuary [ˈmɔːtʃərɪ] *n.* 停尸间
purchase [ˈpɜːtʃəs] *v.* 购买
expensive [ɪkˈspensɪv] *adj.* 昂贵的
exhume [eksˈhjuːm] *v.* 掘出（尸体以检验）
casket [ˈkɑːskɪt] *n.* 棺材
warranty [ˈwɒrəntɪ] *n.* 保修期

# Excellent Skills
# 绝妙的技巧

1 After friends of mine landed at busy Newark Airport, they were unable to attract the attention of any porters to help with their luggage. In desperation, the husband took out a five-dollar bill and waved it above the crowd.

2 In an instant, a skycap was at his side. "Sir," observed the porter, "you certainly have excellent communication skills."

点睛译文

1 我的朋友们在繁忙的纽瓦克机场着陆后，却不能招呼到脚夫来帮他们搬行李。无奈，丈夫拿出一张 5 美元的钞票在人群上方摇晃。

2 一个脚夫马上来到他身边。"先生，" 脚夫说道，"很明显你有绝妙的交际技巧。"

生词宝库

land [lænd] *v.* 登陆，到达

attract [əˈtrækt] *v.* 吸引

porter [ˈpɔːtə] *n.* 搬运工

luggage [ˈlʌɡɪdʒ] *n.* 行李

desperation [despəˈreɪʃn] *n.* 绝望的境地

wave [weɪv] *v.* 挥舞

skycap [ˈskaɪkæp] *n.* 机场行李搬运工

communication [kəmjuːnɪˈkeɪʃən] *n.* 交流；沟通

# A Thank-you Note
# 一封感谢信

## 点睛译文

1 有一次，我收到一封感谢信，是一个我曾帮助过的朋友寄来的。信封内有5张彩票，都被刮过了，露出了数字。

2 “非常感谢您的帮助，”信上写道，“作为礼物，我给您买了些彩票——真遗憾，您没中奖。”

## 爆笑故事

1 Once I received a thank-you note from a friend whom I had helped. In the envelope were five lottery tickets that had been scratched, revealing the numbers.

2 “Thank you very much for your help,” the note read. “As a gift, I bought you some lottery tickets – sorry you didn’t win.”

## 生词宝库

thank-you note 感谢信

lottery [ˈlɒtərɪ] *n.* 彩票

reveal [rɪˈviːl] *v.* 显示

gift [gɪft] *n.* 礼物

# Visual Training
# 视力训练

1 The squad was having "visual training".

2 One smart recruit was asked by the officer to count how many men composed a digging party in a distant field. The party was so far away that the men appeared as mere dots, but unhesitatingly the recruit replied: "Sixteen men and a sergeant, sir."

3 "Right, but how do you know there's a sergeant there？ "

4 "He's not doing any digging, sir."

点睛译文

1 班里正在进行"视力训练"。

2 一个聪明伶俐的新兵被班长叫出来数远处旷野上挖掘队里的人数。采掘队在很远的地方，那些人看起来只是一些小点儿，但是这个新兵毫不犹豫地回答："16 个兵外加 1 个中士，长官。"

3 "正确，可是你怎么知道那儿有 1 个中士？ "

4 "他不干活，长官。"

生词宝库

squad [skwɒd] *n.* 班
visual [ˈvɪʒʊəl] *adj.* 视觉的
recruit [rɪˈkruːt] *n.* 新兵
compose [kəmˈpəʊz] *v.* 构成；组成
digging [ˈdɪɡɪŋ] *n.* 挖掘
unhesitatingly [ʌnˈhezɪteɪtɪŋlɪ] *adv.* 不踌躇地
sergeant [ˈsɑːdʒənt] *n.* 中士；军士

# Mushroom and Toadstool

# 蘑菇与毒蕈

1 Younger Scout: How can I tell the difference between a mushroom and a toadstool?

2 Older Scout: Just eat one before you go to bed. If you wake up the next morning, it was a mushroom.

1 年少的侦察兵：我怎样才能把蘑菇和毒蕈区别开呢？

2 年长的侦察兵：上床前吃一个。如果你第二天早上醒过来了，那就是蘑菇。

生词宝库

Scout [skaʊt] *n.* 侦察兵

mushroom [ˈmʌʃrʊm] *n.* 蘑菇

toadstool [ˈtəʊdstuːl] *n.* 毒蕈

wake up 醒来

# When a Tiger Comes

# 老虎来了

1 Two guys were walking through the jungle. All of a sudden, a tiger appeared from a distance, running towards them. One of the guys took out a pair of Nikes from his bag and started to put them on. The other guy look at him in surprise and exclaimed, "Do you think you will run faster than the tiger with those?"

2 His friend replied, "I don't have to outrun it; I just have to run faster than you."

点睛译文

1 两个男人正在穿过丛林，突然，一只老虎出现在远处，向他们冲来。当中的一个人从包里拿出一双耐克跑鞋开始穿。另一个人惊奇地看着他说，"你以为穿上跑鞋就可以跑得过老虎吗？"

2 他的朋友回答道："我不用跑得过它，我只要跑得比你快就行了。"

生词宝库

jungle [ˈdʒʌŋgl] *n.* 丛林
sudden [ˈsʌdn] *n.* 突发之事
tiger [ˈtaɪgə] *n.* 老虎
distance [ˈdɪstəns] *n.* 远处
pair [peə] *n.* 一对；一双；
outrun [aʊtˈrʌn] *v.* 超过；跑得比……快

# The King's Brother
# 国王的兄弟

## 点睛译文

1 一个穷汉去见西班牙国王，说自己是他的兄弟，求他施恩周济。国王想知道他何以攀认亲戚，穷汉回答说，“我们有共同的祖先——亚当和夏娃。”

2 听了这话，国王就给了他一个小铜子儿。

3 于是穷人开始叫屈，说：“难道您国王陛下就给兄弟这么一点点钱吗？”

4 “走开，快走，”国王回答，“如果世界上你所有的兄弟们都像我这样给你一个铜板，你就比我还有钱了。”

## 爆笑故事

1 A poor man, presenting himself before the King of Spain, asked his charity, telling him that he was his brother. The king wanted to know how he claimed kindred to him. The poor fellow replied, “We are all descended from one common father and mother, viz., Adam and Eve.”

2 Upon which the king gave him a little copper piece of money.

3 The poor man began to bemoan himself, saying, “Is it possible that your Majesty should give no more than this to your brother?”

4 “Away, away.” replies the king, “if all the brothers you have in the world give you as much as I have done, you'll be richer than I am.”

## 生词宝库

present [ˈpreznt] *v.* 介绍

kindred [ˈkɪndrəd] *adj.* 有血缘关系的

descend [dɪˈsend] *v.* 来自；是……的后裔

common [ˈkɒmən] *adj.* 共同的

copper [ˈkɒpə] *n.* 铜币

bemoan [bɪˈməʊn] *v.* 悲叹

# Three Men in a Boat
# 三人同舟

## 爆笑故事

1 Three men were sitting on a park bench. The one in the middle was reading a newspaper; the others were pretending to fish. They baited imaginary hooks, cast lines and reeled in their catch.

2 A passing policeman stopped to watch the spectacle and asked the man in the middle if he knew the other two.

3 "Oh yes." he said. "They are my friends."

4 "In that case," warned the officer, "you'd better get them out of here!"

5 "Yes, sir." the man replied, and he began rowing furiously.

## 点睛译文

1 三个男子在公园的长椅上坐着。中间的一个在读报纸，另外两个假装在钓鱼，他们给想象中的鱼钩上鱼饵，放线，并卷线把鱼抓上来。

2 一位过路警察驻足观察了这个景象，他问中间的那个男子是否认识其他两位。

3 "喔，认识。" 他说，"他们是我的朋友。"

4 "那样的话。" 警察告诫说，"你最好把他们从这里弄走。"

5 "好的，警官。" 那男子回答说，接着就开始疯狂地做起划桨的动作来。

## 生词宝库

bench [bentʃ] *n.* 长凳

bait [beɪt] *v.* 引……上钩

imaginary [ɪˈmædʒɪnərɪ] *adj.* 想象的

hook [hʊk] *n.* 钓鱼钩

cast [kɑːst] *v.* 投，抛

reel [riːl] *v.* 卷

spectacle [ˈspektəkəl] *n.* 景象；场面

furiously [ˈfjʊərɪəslɪ] *adv.* 疯狂地；猛烈地

# The Choice of Word

# 选词

1 一天下班回家，约翰发现妻子在摇半岁的女儿，嘴里对小婴儿反复念道：“爸——爸。”约翰心里感到美滋滋的，因为他的妻子首先选择了“爸爸”这个词教给孩子。

2 几周后的一天夜里，约翰和妻子被一阵哭声惊醒了。“爸爸！”

3 “她在叫你，亲爱的。”妻子说，然后翻身竟自睡了。

1 One day, John was back home after work. He found that his wife was shaking their daughter who was only half a year old. She said “Da-Dy” to the baby many times. John felt very happy because he thought his wife chose the word “Dady” to teach their baby.

2 During one night several weeks later, John and his wife were wakened up by the cry “Dady”.

3 His wife said to him, “Darling, she is calling you.” Then she turned to sleep.

choose [tʃuːz] *v.* 选择

several [ˈsevrəl] *adj.* 几个的

waken [ˈweɪkən] *v.* 唤醒

darling [ˈdɑːlɪŋ] *n.* 亲爱的

# Day after Day

# 日复一日

## 爆笑故事

1 A teacher was always so involved in the text being studied that he never looked up. He would call on a student for translation and explanation, and — without realizing it — he often chose the same student day after day. Out of respect, the student wouldn't point this out to him.

2 After being called on four days in a row, a student named Goldberg asked advice from his friends.

3 The next day when the teacher said, "Goldberg, translate and explain."

4 Goldberg replied: "Goldberg is absent today."

5 "All right," said the teacher. "You translate and explain."

## 点睛译文

1 一位老师对所讲课文总是非常投入，从不抬头。他常让一个学生来翻译和解释，并且居然没意识到他常常日复一日地叫同一个学生。出于尊敬，学生并没有给他指出这一点。

2 一个叫戈德堡的学生，在被一连叫了4天之后，向他的朋友寻求建议。

3 第二天，这位教师又说："戈德堡，翻译并解释。"

4 戈德堡回答说："戈德堡今天缺席。"

5 "那好吧，"教师说，"那就你来翻译并解释。"

## 生词宝库

translation [træns'leɪʃn] *n.* 翻译

explanation [ˌeksplə'neɪʃn] *n.* 解释

realize ['riːəlaɪz] *v.* 认识到

respect [rɪ'spekt] *n.* 尊敬

advice [əd'vaɪs] *n.* 建议

absent ['æbsənt] *adj.* 缺席的

# Keep Feeding Him Nickels 再喂他几枚5分镍币

## 爆笑故事

1 A mother saw her three-year-old son put nickel in his mouth and swallowed it. She immediately picked him up, turned him upside down and hit him on the back, whereupon he coughed up two dimes. Frantically, she called to the father outside, "Your son just swallowed a nickel and coughed up two dimes! What shall I do?"

2 Yelled back the father, "Keep feeding him nickels!"

## 点睛译文

1 母亲见3岁的儿子将一枚5分镍币放进嘴里吞了下去，她立刻将他抱起，头朝下不停地拍打他的后背，他咳出了两枚一角的硬币。她发狂似的朝正在外面的孩子父亲喊道："你儿子刚才吞下了一枚5分镍币，可咳出两枚一角的硬币！我该怎么办呢？"

2 孩子他爸大声回答道："再喂他几枚镍币！"

## 生词宝库

nickel [ˈnɪkl] *n.* 五分镍币

immediately [ɪˈmiːdɪətlɪ] *adv.* 立即

whereupon [ˌweərəˈpɒn] *conj.* 于是

cough [kɒf] *v.* 咳嗽

# Roast Pig
# 烤乳猪

爆笑故事

1 A gentleman was invited for dinner. When he hurried there and sat down, he was happy to see a roast pig in front of his seat and said, "Not bad, I am next to the pig."

2 But then he noticed the angry fat lady sitting next to him. He faked a smile and added, "Oh I am sorry; I meant the roasted one on the table."

点睛译文

1 一位先生去赴宴，匆忙入座后，发现自己的座位正对着乳猪，于是大为高兴地说："还不错，我坐在乳猪的旁边。"

2 这时才发现身旁的一位胖女士正对他怒目而视，他忙陪笑改口道："哦，对不起，我说的是桌上那只烤好的。"

生词宝库

invite [ɪnˈvaɪt] *v.* 邀请
hurry [ˈhʌrɪ] *v.* 急赶
roast [rəʊst] *adj.* 烘烤的
fat [fæt] *adj.* 肥胖的
fake [feɪk] *v.* 假装；做假动作
add [æd] *v.* 加

# A Vacation Cruise

# 假日巡航游

1 一个愚笨之人读到一则假日巡航游只须花100元的广告。在他签字付款后，旅游经纪人用棒猛击了他一下，把他打昏了过去，并把他从后门扔进了河里。不久又来了一个人，付了钱并得到了相同的待遇。

2 15分钟后，这两个人一起向河的下游漂去。第一个人说："不知道他们这次巡航游是否提供食物。"

3 "不知道，"第二个人说道，"去年是没有的。"

1 One stupid guy reads an ad about a vacation cruise that costs only $100. After he signs up and pays, the travel agent hits him with a bat, knocks him unconscious and throws him out the back door into the river. Soon another guy comes in, pays his fee and gets the same treatment.

2 Fifteen minutes later, as the two are floating down the river together, the first man says, "I wonder if they're serving any food on this cruise."

3 "I don't know," the second guy replied, "They didn't last year."

## 生词宝库

vacation [vəˈkeɪʃn] *n.* 假期
cruise [kruːz] *v.* 乘船游览
agent [ˈeɪdʒənt] *n.* 代理商
bat [bæt] *n.* 球棒
knock [nɒk] *v.* 敲
treatment [ˈtriːtmənt] *n.* 对待
float [fləʊt] *v.* 漂浮

# A Girl's Name
# 女孩的名字

1 When our daughter was born, we named her Myles, after my beloved late father, despite family warning that the name was too masculine.

2 Years later, when I felt she was old enough to understand, I explained to Myles, "Your name is very special. I named you after my own father because I loved him very much. I know he would be proud of you."

3 Myles thought carefully about this and then said, "I know all that, Mom. But I don't understand why my grandfather had a girl's name."

1 女儿出生时，我们给她取名叫迈尔斯，和我深爱的已过世的父亲同一个名字，不过家人提醒这个名字太男性化了。

2 几年以后，我觉得迈尔斯已经长大，能够懂事了。我对她解释说："你的名字很特别。我给你取了一个和我爸爸一样的名字，因为我非常爱他。我相信他会为你而深感自豪的。"

3 迈尔斯很仔细地想了一下，然后说道："这些我都懂，妈妈。可是我不知道外公为什么会有一个女孩子的名字。"

## 生词宝库

beloved [bɪˈlʌvɪd] *adj.* 心爱的

despite [dɪˈspaɪt] *prep.* 尽管，不管

masculine [ˈmæskjʊlɪn] *adj.* 男性的

proud [praʊd] *adj.* 自豪的

# The Sun and the Moon
# 太阳和月亮

1 两个男孩在谈论太阳和月亮。

2 “它们中哪个更有用？”其中一个问道。

3 “当然是月亮。月亮在天黑时挂在天空，但太阳是在白天谁也不需要它的时候挂在天上的。”

1 Two boys are talking about the sun and the moon.

2 “Which one of them is more useful?” asked one of them.

3 “Of course the moon is. The moon is in the sky when it’s dark, but the sun is in the sky in the daytime when nobody needs it.”

## 词汇无障碍

sun [sʌn] *n.* 太阳

moon [muːn] *n.* 月亮

useful [ˈjuːsfl] *adj.* 有用的

daytime [ˈdeɪtaɪm] *n.* 白天

nobody [ˈnəʊbədɪ] *pron.* 没有人

# Twenty $1
# 20张一美元

## 爆笑故事

1 A lady lost her handbag in the bustle of Christmas shopping. It was found by an honest boy and returned to her.

2 Looking in her purse, she commented, “Hmmm... That’s funny. When I lost my purse there was a $20 bill in it. Now there are twenty $1 bills.”

3 The boy quickly replied, “That’s right, lady. The last time I found a lady’s purse, she didn’t have any change for a reward.”

## 点睛译文

1 一位女士圣诞节购物时丢了钱包。一个诚实的小男孩捡到了钱包，还给了她。

2 她看了看钱包，说：“嗯……真有趣。我丢钱包时，里面有一张20元的钞票。现在却有20张一元的钞票。”

3 那个男孩马上回答说：“没错，太太。上次我捡到一位女士的钱包，她没有零钱酬谢。”

## 生词宝库

handbag [ˈhændbæg] *n.* 手提包

bustle [ˈbʌsl] *n.* 喧哗

honest [ˈɒnɪst] *adj.* 诚实的

comment [ˈkɒment] *v.* 发表意见

purse [pɜːs] *n.* 钱包（女士）

reward [rɪˈwɔːd] *n.* 酬谢

# He's Taking the Picture
# 他正在拍照

1 姐妹俩在看一本宗教画册时，刚好看到一幅圣母玛利亚和圣婴耶稣的图画。

2 姐姐说："瞧，这是耶稣，这是他的妈妈。"

3 "他的爸爸在哪里？"妹妹想知道。

4 姐姐想了一会儿，解释道："噢，他正在拍照。"

1 Two sisters were looking at a book of religious pictures and came across a painting of the Virgin and the baby Jesus.

2 "See there," said the older sister, "that's Jesus, and that's his mother.

3 "Where's his dad?" the younger girl wanted to know.

4 Her sister thought for a moment and explained, "Oh, he's taking the picture."

## 生词宝库

religious [rɪˈlɪdʒəs] *adj.* 宗教的

picture [ˈpɪktʃə] *n.* 绘画作品

virgin [ˈvɜːdʒɪn] *n.* 圣母玛利亚；处女

Jesus [ˈdʒiːzəs] *n.* 耶稣

# A Picture of God
# 一幅上帝的画像

1 "I'm going to draw a picture of God," a four-year-old girl said to her teacher.

2 "But nobody knows what God looks like." the teacher said.

3 "They will know when I've finished." came the reply.

点睛译文

1 一个4岁的女孩对老师说："我要画一幅上帝的画像。"

2 老师说："可谁也不知道上帝长什么模样。"

3 "等我画好后他们就会知道的。"小女孩回答说。

生词宝库

draw [drɔː] *v.* 画

God [gɒd] *n.* 上帝

# What's His Number?
# 他的号码多少？

## 点睛译文

1 每个星期日，牧师给孩子们讲故事时，都会把他们叫到教堂前面。有一次，为了更好地阐述祈祷的含义，他带来了一部电话。

2 “你们和别人在电话里交谈，看不到电话另一端的人，对吗？”他开口问道。

3 孩子们点头称是。

4 “嗯，和上帝交谈，就像在电话里交谈一样。他在另一端，但你看不到他。不过，他在听。”

5 就在这时，一个小男孩尖着嗓子问道：“他的号码是多少？”

## 爆笑故事

1 Each Sunday the minister called the children to the front of the church while he told them a story. Once he brought a telephone to better illustrate the idea of prayer.

2 “You talk to people on the telephone and don’t see them on the other end of the line, right?” he began.

3 The children nodded yes.

4 “Well, talking to God is like talking on the telephone. He’s on the other end, but you can’t see him. He is listening, though.”

5 Just then, a little boy piped up and asked, “What’s his number?”

## 生词宝库

minister [ˈmɪnɪstə] *n.* 牧师

church [tʃɜːtʃ] *n.* 教堂

illustrate [ˈɪləstreɪt] *v.* 阐明

prayer [preə] *n.* 祈祷

nod [nɒd] *v.* 点头

pipe [paɪp] *v.* 尖叫

# Good Sight
# 好视力

## 爆笑故事

1 Lawyer: You say you were about thirty-five feet away from the scene of the accident? Just how far can you see clearly?

2 Witness: Well, when I wake up in the morning I see the sun, and they tell me it's about ninety-three million miles away.

## 点睛译文

1 律师：你说你离事故现场约有 35 英尺，你能看清多远的东西？

2 证人：这么说吧，早上起床后我看见太阳，别人告诉我这大约有 9300 万英里远。

feet [fiːt] *n.* 英尺

scene [siːn] *n.* 情景

clearly [ˈklɪəlɪ] *adv.* 清晰地

million [ˈmɪljən] *n.* 百万

# Each Must Be Good

# 每个都是好的

## 点睛译文

1 有一个人爱钱甚于一切。

2 一天，他派儿子去买一盒火柴，并告诉儿子每根火柴都必须是好的。儿子一会儿就回来了。那人掏出火柴，划了一根，没有燃着。他又划了几根，还是无济于事。他非常生气，说道："我不是告诉你每根火柴都必须是好的吗？"

3 "是的，你说过，"男孩说道，"我把盒子里所有的火柴都试过了，每一根都能划着。"

## 爆笑故事

1 There was a man who cared more for money than anything else.

2 One day he sent his son to buy a box of matches, and told the boy he must see that each match in the box was good. Soon the boy came back. The man took out a match and struck it, but it failed to light. He tried several more, but in vain. He got so angry and said, "I told you each match must be good, didn't I?"

3 "Yes, you did," the boy replied, "I tried out all the matches in the box and each match lit."

## 生词宝库

anything [ˈenɪθɪŋ] pron. 任何事

match [mætʃ] n. 火柴

fail [feɪl] v. 失败

in vain [ɪn veɪn] 徒劳

# The Train
# 火车

## 爆笑故事

1 The buddy said to Tom, "I hear that it's the safest sitting in the middle of the train. Once an accident occurs, both ends of the train get damaged worst."

2 "Idiot! Why won't they get rid of both ends of the train?"

## 点睛译文

1 伙伴对汤姆说："我听说坐在火车中间最安全。一旦发生事故，火车两头遭到的破坏最大。"

2 "白痴！他们为什么不去掉火车的两头呢？"

## 词汇无障碍

buddy [ˈbʌdɪ] *n.* 伙伴

middle [ˈmɪdl] *n.* 中间

damage [ˈdæmɪdʒ] *v.* 毁坏

idiot [ˈɪdɪət] *n.* 白痴

# Save Money
# 省钱

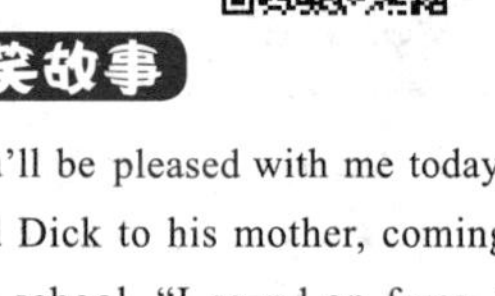

1 “妈妈，你今天会对我满意的。”放学回家后，迪克对妈妈说，“我省下了车钱。我上学时没有乘公共汽车，而是一路跟着公共汽车跑去的。”

2 “噢，”她的妈妈笑道，“下次你应该跟在出租车后面跑，会省更多。”

1 “You’ll be pleased with me today, mom.” said Dick to his mother, coming home from school. “I saved on fares. I didn’t go to school by bus but ran all the way after it.”

2 “Well,” said his mother laughing, “Next time you should run after a taxi, you’ll save much more.”

## 生词宝库

pleased [pli:zd] *adj.* 高兴的；满意的

save [seɪv] *v.* 节省

fare [feə] *n.* 车费

laugh [lɑ:f] *v.* 笑

taxi [ˈtæksɪ] *n.* 出租车

# Put It Up Again
# 重新挂上去

1 The orchard-keeper spotted a little boy sneaks into the orchard and climbs an apple tree, so he raced over.

2 "Little devil, what are you doing up on my tree?"

3 "Look here, sir, an apple fell off your tree, so I'm trying to put it up again!" the boy replied holding the apple in his hand.

点睛译文

1 护园人发现一个小男孩偷偷钻进果园，爬上了一棵苹果树，就迅速走了过去。

2 "小家伙，你在我的树上做什么？"

3 "看这里，先生，一个苹果从您的树上掉了下来，所以我想把它重新挂上去！"小男孩举着手里的苹果回答说。

生词宝库

sneak [sniːk] *v.* 偷偷地走
orchard [ˈɔːtʃəd] *n.* 果园
climb [klaɪm] *v.* 爬
race [reɪs] *v.* 急走
fell [fel] *v.* 落下（动词 fall 的过去式）

# Write It Loudly

# 写得大声点

1 “你有没有照我说的那样给爷爷写感谢信？”

2 “有，妈妈。”简回答说。

3 “你的字写得好像很大。”

4 “啊，爷爷耳聋，所以我要写得大声点。”

## 爆笑故事

1 “Are you writing a thank-you letter to Grandpa like I told you?”

2 “Yes, mama.” replied Jane.

3 “Your handwriting seems very large.”

4 “Well, Grandpa’s deaf, so I’m writing it loudly.”

## 生词宝库

handwriting [ˈhændraɪtɪŋ] *n.* 笔迹

seem [siːm] *v.* 似乎；好像

loudly [laʊdlɪ] *adv.* 大声地

# Give Me a Dollar
# 给我一块钱

1 Son: Dad, give me a dime.

2 Father: Son, don't you think you're getting too big to be forever begging for dimes?

3 Son: I guess you're right, dad. Give me a dollar, will you?

1 儿子：爸爸，给我一毛钱。

2 父亲：儿子，你不认为自己渐渐长大了，不应该总是一毛钱一毛钱地要了吗？

3 儿子：爸爸，我想你说得对。给我一块钱，好吗？

## 生词宝库

forever [fər'evə] *adv.* 永远

beg [beg] *v.* 要求

guess [ges] *v.* 猜想

dollar ['dɒlə] *n.* 美元

# He Won

# 他赢了

1 汤米：约翰尼，你的弟弟好吗？

2 约翰尼：他卧病在床，他伤着了自己。

3 汤米：太糟了。是怎么回事？

4 约翰尼：我们做游戏，看谁能把身子探出窗外最远，结果他赢了。

1 Tommy: How is your little brother, Johnny?

2 Johnny: He is ill in bed. He hurt himself.

3 Tommy: That's too bad. How did that happen?

4 Johnny: We played who could lean furthest out of the window, and he won.

hurt [hɜːt] *v.* 伤害

happen [ˈhæpən] *v.* 发生

furthest [ˈfɜːðɪst] *adv.* 最远

win [wɪn] *v.* 赢；获胜

# I'll Learn the Latter Half

# 我就学后半部分

## 爆笑故事

1 Son: Dad, is French hard to learn?

2 Father: My boy, at the beginning it is, but after that, it becomes easy.

3 Son: That's great! I'll learn the latter half.

## 点睛译文

1 儿子：爸爸，法语难学吗？

2 父亲：我的孩子，开头难，但往后就变得容易了。

3 儿子：太棒了！那我就学后半部分。

## 生词宝库

French [frentʃ] *n.* 法语

learn [lɜːn] *v.* 学习

easy [ˈiːzɪ] *adj.* 容易的

latter [ˈlætə] *adj.* 较后的

# Lost Way
# 迷路

## 点睛译文

1 一个小孩迷了路，就去问路边的警察。

2 警察问："小家伙，你的家在哪里？"

3 男孩回答说："妈妈教我迷路时，就去问警察，但她没有告诉我住在哪里。"

## 爆笑故事

1 A little boy lost his way and went to ask the policeman by the road.

2 The policeman asked, "Sonny, where's your home?"

3 The boy replied, "My mother teaches me to ask the policeman when I lose my way, but she doesn't tell me where I live."

## 生词宝库

lose one's way 迷路

road [rəʊd] *n.* 路

ask [ɑːsk] *v.* 询问

live [lɪv] *v.* 居住

# Chocolate Car

# 巧克力车

## 爆笑故事

1 The mother asked her little son, "Tom, if the car is made of chocolate, which part will you eat first?

2 Tom replied quickly, "Wheels! Then the car won't be off."

## 点睛译文

1 一母亲问小儿子："汤姆，如果汽车是用巧克力做的，你先吃哪部分？"

2 汤姆飞快地答道："轮子！这样汽车就开不走了。"

## 生词宝库

little [ˈlɪtl] *adj.* 幼小的

chocolate [ˈtʃɒkələt] *n.* 巧克力

part [pɑːt] *n.* 部分

quickly [ˈkwɪklɪ] *adv.* 迅速地

# Lucky Mother

# 幸运的母亲

## 点睛译文

1 一位年轻的母亲认为，世界上还有许多忍饥挨饿的人，浪费食物真不应该。

2 有天晚上，在安排年幼的女儿睡觉之前，她给女儿喂夜宵。她先给她一片新鲜的黑面包和黄油，但孩子说她不喜欢这样吃。她还要在面包上涂一些果酱。

3 母亲看了女儿几秒钟，随即说道："露茜，当我像你一样小的时候，总是吃面包加黄油，或者面包加果酱，从来没有在面包上既加黄油又加果酱。"

4 露茜看了母亲一会儿，眼中露出怜悯的神情，然后她柔声说："您现在能跟我们生活在一起难道不感到高兴吗？"

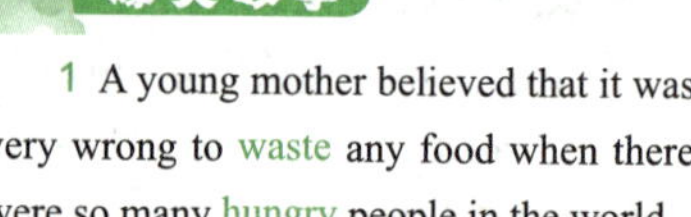

## 爆笑故事

1 A young mother believed that it was very wrong to waste any food when there were so many hungry people in the world.

2 One evening, she was giving her small daughter her tea before putting her to bed. First she gave her a slice of fresh brown bread and butter, but the child said that she did not want it like that. She asked for some jam on her bread as well.

3 Her mother looked at her for a few seconds and then said, "When I was a small girl like you, Lucy, I was always given either bread and butter, or bread and jam, but never bread with butter and jam."

4 Lucy looked at her mother for a few moments with pity in her eyes and then said to her kindly, "Aren't you pleased that you've come to live with us now?"

## 生词宝库

waste [weɪst] *v.* 浪费

hungry [ˈhʌŋgrɪ] *adj.* 饥饿的

slice [slaɪs] *n.* 薄片

butter [ˈbʌtə] *n.* 黄油

jam [dʒæm] *n.* 果酱

pity [ˈpɪtɪ] *n.* 怜悯，同情

# I'm Trying to Copy Him

# 跟他学

## 爆笑故事

1 Nurse: Don't you like your new baby sister, Johnny?

2 Johnny: She's all right, but I wish she had been a boy. Willie Smith had just got a new sister, and now he'll think I'm trying to copy him.

## 点睛译文

1 保姆：约翰尼，你不喜欢新出生的小妹妹吗？

2 约翰尼：她还可以，但她要是一个男孩就好了。威利·史密斯刚有一个新出生的小妹妹，现在他会认为我是想跟他学。

## 生词宝库

new [njuː] *adj.* 新的

wish [wɪʃ] *v.* 希望

sister [ˈsɪstə] *n.* 姐妹

copy [ˈkɒpɪ] *v.* 模仿

# Take the Medicine

# 吃药

## 点睛译文

1 米奇拒绝吃药，于是他的妈妈吓唬他说："赶快吃下去，不然我就去叫警察。"

2 "妈妈，警察喜欢吃药吗？"米奇好奇地问道。

## 爆笑故事

1 Mickey refused to take the medicine, so his mother swashed him and said, "Hurry to take it down, or I'll call the police."

2 "Does the police like to take the medicine, mama?" Mickey asked curiously.

## 生词宝库

refuse [rɪ'fju:z] *v.* 拒绝

medicine ['medsən] *n.* 药

swash [swɒʃ] *v.* 吓唬

curiously ['kjʊərɪəslɪ] *adv.* 好奇地

# Welcome to McDonald's
# 欢迎光临麦当劳

## 爆笑故事

1 On the way to preschool, the doctor had left her stethoscope on the car seat, and her little girl picked it up and began playing with it.

2 "Well, my daughter wants to follow in my footsteps!" thought the doctor.

3 Then the child spoke into the instrument, "Welcome to McDonald's. May I take your order?"

## 点睛译文

1 在去幼儿园的路上，一个医生把听诊器留在了车座上。她的小女儿拿起听诊器玩了起来。

2 "看来女儿想接我的班！"医生想道。

3 接着，小女孩对着听诊器说道："欢迎光临麦当劳。您要点什么？"

## 生词宝库

preschool [ˈpriːskuːl] *n.* 幼稚园

stethoscope [ˈsteθəskəʊp] *n.* 听诊器

footstep [ˈfʊtstep] *n.* 脚步

instrument [ˈɪnstrəmənt] *n.* 器械

# You Can Stand Aside
# 你可以躲开

1 一个男孩吃了很多饼干，但还想吃。

2 他的父亲对他说：“不要再吃了，不然你的肚子就会撑爆的。”

3 男孩说：“不要紧。我再吃时，你可以躲开。”

## 爆笑故事

1 A boy had eaten a lot of cookies, but he wanted more.

2 His father said to him, “Don’t eat any more, or your stomach will explode.”

3 The boy said, “Never mind. When I’m eating once again, you can stand aside.”

## 生词宝库

eat [iːt] *v.* 吃

stomach [ˈstʌmək] *n.* 胃

explode [ɪkˈspləʊd] *v.* 爆炸

aside [əˈsaɪd] *adv.* 在一边

# Apples have Gone to Bed

# 苹果已经睡觉了

## 爆笑故事

1 It was so late. Frank lay in bed and demanded his mother to peel the apple for him.

2 "It's so late, sonny, that apples have already gone to bed."

3 "No, they won't, mama. The small apples may have gone to bed, but the big ones mustn't."

## 点睛译文

1 天很晚了。弗兰克躺在床上，要妈妈给他削苹果吃。

2 "孩子，太晚了，苹果已经睡觉了。"

3 "不，不会的，妈妈。小苹果可能睡了，但大苹果一定没有睡。"

## 生词宝库

late [leɪt] *adj.* 晚的

lay [leɪ] *v.* 躺下（lie 的过去式）

demand [dɪˈmɑːnd] *v.* 要求，请求

peel [piːl] *v.* 削去……的皮

# The Night Will Come Inside 黑夜会进来

1 吉米 3 岁了。

2 一天，他正在窗口观望，夜幕降临。他突然喊道：“妈妈，妈妈，快来关窗！”

3 “为什么？天不冷呀，宝贝。”

4 “是的，妈妈，可黑夜会进来。”

1 Jimmy is three years old.

2 One day, he was gazing out of the window when the night fell. He suddenly shouted, “Mum, mum, come close the window!”

3 “Why? It’s not cold, sonny.”

4 “Yes, mum, but the night will come inside.”

gaze [geɪz] *v.* 凝视

shout [ʃaʊt] *v.* 呼喊

cold [kəʊld] *adj.* 冷的

inside [ˌɪnˈsaɪd] *adv.* 在里面

# He's a Barber
# 他是一名理发师

## 爆笑故事

1 Harry: My big brother shaves every day.

2 Henry: My brother shaves fifty times a day.

3 Harry: Is he crazy?

4 Henry: No, he's a barber.

## 点睛译文

1 哈里：我哥哥每天都刮脸。

2 亨利：我哥哥每天刮50次脸。

3 哈里：他疯了吗？

4 亨利：没有，他是一名理发师。

## 生词宝库

shave [ʃeɪv] *v.* 剃（头发、胡须）

time [taɪm] *n.* 次

crazy [ˈkreɪzɪ] *adj.* 疯狂的

barber [ˈbɑːbə] *n.* 理发师

# The Thinker
# 《思考者》

## 点睛译文

1 两个男孩正在欣赏罗丹的著名雕塑《思考者》。

2 “你猜他在想什么？”其中一个问道。

3 “我猜他是在想他把衣服放哪里了吧。”另一个回答说。

## 爆笑故事

1 Two boys were admiring the famous statue by Rodin entitled *The Thinker*.

2 “What do you suppose he’s thinking about?” asked one.

3 “I guess he’s thinking about where he put his clothes.” replied the other.

## 生词宝库

admire [əd'maɪə] *v.* 欣赏

famous ['feɪməs] *adj.* 著名的

statue ['stætʃuː] *n.* 雕像

entitle [ɪn'taɪtl] *v.* 取名为

suppose [sə'pəuz] *v.* 猜想

clothes [kləuz] *n.* 衣服

# Write a Letter
# 写信

## 爆笑故事

1 Milly: What are you doing?

2 Molly: I'm writing a letter to myself.

3 Milly: What does it say?

4 Molly: How do I know? I won't get it till tomorrow.

## 点睛译文

1 米丽：你在做什么？

2 茉莉：我在给自己写信。

3 米丽：信上说什么？

4 茉莉：我怎么知道？我到明天才会收到。

## 生词宝库

myself [maɪ'self] pron. 我自己

till [tɪl] prep. 直到

tomorrow [tə'mɒrəʊ] n. 明天；未来

# Is Ink So Expensive
# 墨水很贵吗

## 爆笑故事

1 "Is ink so expensive, daddy?"

2 "Why, no, what makes you think so?"

3 "Well. Mother seems quite disturbed because I spilled some ink on the carpet."

## 点睛译文

1 "墨水很贵吗，爸爸？"

2 "啊，不贵，你为什么这样想？ "

3 "啊。我把一些墨水洒到了地毯上，妈妈好像很难过。"

## 生词宝库

think [θɪŋk] *v.* 认为

disturbed [dɪˈstɜːbd] *adj.* 不安的

ink [ɪŋk] *n.* 墨水

carpet [ˈkɑːpɪt] *n.* 地毯

# That's What I've Been Doing 我一直都是这样做的

1 A mother was talking to her little boy.

2 "Now, Billy, you shouldn't be selfish with your toys. I've told you to let your younger brother play with them half the time."

3 "That's what I've been doing." said Billy, "I take the sled doing downhill, and he takes it going up."

1 一位母亲在和她的小男孩说话。

2 "听着，比利，你不应该吝啬自己的玩具。我已经对你说过要让弟弟玩一半的时间。"

3 "我一直都是这样做的。"比利说，"我把雪橇滑下坡，他再拿上来。"

生词宝库

selfish [ˈselfɪʃ] *adj.* 自私的

toy [tɒɪ] *n.* 玩具

younger [ˈjʌŋgə] *adj.* 较年轻的

sled [sled] *n.* <美> 雪撬

downhill [ˌdaʊnˈhɪl] *adv.* 向山下；走下坡路地

# A Scarecrow
# 稻草人

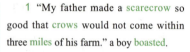

1 一个男孩夸口说："我爸爸做的稻草人非常好，所以他的农场3英里内都没有乌鸦。"

2 "那有什么。"他的朋友说："我叔叔做的稻草人非常棒，乌鸦把去年偷的所有粮食都送了回来。"

1 "My father made a scarecrow so good that crows would not come within three miles of his farm." a boy boasted.

2 "That's nothing." his friend said, "My uncle made a scarecrow so good that the crows brought back all the corn they had stolen the previous years."

## 生词宝库

scarecrow [ˈskeəkrəʊ] *n.* 稻草人

crow [krəʊ] *n.* 乌鸦

mile [maɪl] *n.* 英里

boast [bəʊst] *v.* 自夸；吹牛

# The Elephants

# 大象

## 爆笑故事

1 A small girl was telling her friend all about her first time to the zoo.

2 "And I saw the elephants," she said, "and what do you think they were doing? Picking up peanuts with their vacuums!"

## 点睛译文

1 一小女孩正把她第一次去动物园的感受告诉她的一位朋友。

2 "我看见了大象，"她说，"你知道它们在干什么吗？正在用真空吸尘器捡花生呢。"

## 生词宝库

zoo [zuː] *n.* 动物园

elephant [ˈelɪfənt] *n.* 大象

vacuum [ˈvækjuəm] *n.* <口> 真空吸尘器

# Are Flies Good to Eat?

# 苍蝇好吃吗？

1 汤米：苍蝇好吃吗？

2 爸爸：我想不好吃。你为什么这样问？

3 汤米：刚才你的馅饼里面有一只。

1 Tommy: Are flies good to eat?

2 Dad: I don't think so. Why do you ask?

3 Tommy: There was one in your pie.

## 生词宝库

fly [flaɪ] *n.* 苍蝇

pie [paɪ] *n.* 馅饼

# The Result of Laziness
# 懒惰的后果

## 爆笑故事

1 Mother: Why were you kept after school today, Johnny?

2 Johnny: Teacher told us to write an essay on "The Result of Laziness", and I turned in a blank sheet of paper.

## 点睛译文

1 妈妈：今天放学后，你为什么会被留下来，约翰尼？

2 约翰尼：老师让我们写一篇作文，题目是《懒惰的后果》，我交了一张白纸。

## 生词宝库

essay [ˈeseɪ] *n.* 文章

laziness [ˈleɪzɪnəs] *n.* 懒惰

blank [blæŋk] *adj.* 空白的

sheet [ʃiːt] *n.* 一张

turn in 上交

# You Are Getting More

# 你有更多了

1 我向脸上抹面霜时，小女儿问我在干什么。我解释说这种面霜对皱纹有好处。

2 她回答说：“妈妈，它肯定很管用。你的皱纹越来越多了。”

1 I was putting cream on my face when my little girl asked what I was doing. I explained that it was good for wrinkles.

2 “It’s sure doing a great job, mommy.” she replied, “You are getting more of them.”

cream [kriːm] *n.* 面霜

explain [ɪkˈspleɪn] *v.* 解释

mommy [ˈmɒmɪ] *n.* 妈咪

# Has No Money to Buy Coke
# 没有钱买可乐

1 Betty: Mama, why does the puppy drink the water in the slot?

2 Mom: Because it's thirsty.

3 Betty: Oh, I know that the puppy has no money to buy coke!

1 贝蒂：妈妈，小狗为什么要喝水沟里的水？

2 妈妈：因为它渴了。

3 贝蒂：噢，我知道了，是小狗没有钱买可乐！

## 生词宝库

puppy [ˈpʌpɪ] *n.* 小狗

slot [slɒt] *n.* 狭缝

thirsty [ˈθɜːstɪ] *adj.* 口渴的

coke [kəʊk] *n.* < 口 > 可口可乐（=Coca-Cola）

# Your Chicken Is in Bloom

# 你的鸡开花了

1 小迈克正在参观爷爷奶奶的农场。他在鸡群中看到一只孔雀。他马上跑向屋子，大声喊道：

2 “奶奶，快来！你的一只鸡开花了！”

1 Little Mike was visiting on his grandparents' farm. Checking the chicken's tail, he came upon a peacock. He ran quickly to the house shouting,

2 "Granny, come quick! Your chicken is in bloom!"

## 生词宝库

farm [fɑːm] *n.* 农场

chicken [ˈtʃɪkɪn] *n.* 鸡

peacock [ˈpiːkɒk] *n.* （雄）孔雀

bloom [bluːm] *n.* 花；绽放

# Have You Weighed Your Boy 称过你儿子了吗

1 Mother: I sent my little boy for two pounds of plums and you gave him a pound and a half.

2 Shopkeeper: My scales are all right, madam. Have you weighed your little boy?

1 母亲：我派自己的小孩买两磅李子，你却给了他一磅半。

2 店主：我的秤没问题，太太。你称过你儿子了吗？

生词宝库

plum [plʌm] *n.* 李子

pound [paʊnd] *n.* 英镑

scale [skeɪl] *n.* 天秤

weigh [weɪ] *v.* 秤重量

# What Are They Doing Here 他们在这里干什么

1 图书管理员走到一个吵闹的小男孩身边，警告说：

2 “请安静！你周围的人都不能读书了！”

3 “不能读书？”小男孩好奇地问道，“那他们在这里干什么？”

1 The librarian went over to a small, noisy boy.

2 “Please be quiet!” she warned. “The people around you can’t read!”

3 “They can’t?” The boy asked curiously. “Then what are they doing here?”

## 生词宝库

librarian [laɪˈbreərɪən] *n.* 图书管理员

noisy [ˈnɔɪzɪ] *adj.* 聒噪的

quiet [ˈkwaɪət] *adj.* 安静的

# Black Hens and White Hens
# 黑母鸡和白母鸡

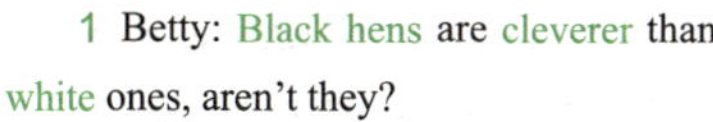

1 Betty: Black hens are cleverer than white ones, aren't they?

2 Larry: How do you know?

3 Betty: Well, the black hens can lay white eggs, but the white hens can't lay black ones.

1 贝蒂：黑母鸡比白母鸡聪明，对吗？

2 拉里：你怎么知道？

3 贝蒂：嗯，因为黑母鸡能下白蛋，可白母鸡不能下黑蛋。

生词宝库

black [blæk] *adj.* 黑色的

hen [hen] *n.* 母鸡

clever [ˈklevə] *adj.* 聪明的

white [waɪt] *adj.* 白色的

lay [leɪ] *v.* 下蛋

egg [eg] *n.* 蛋

# A Pair of New Trousers
# 一条新裤子

## 点睛译文

1 珍妮的爸爸给她新买了一条裤子，但刚一下水就缩得不能穿了。她的妈妈非常生气。

2 珍妮却说：“妈妈，你给我洗个澡，我就能穿了。”

## 爆笑故事

1 Jenny's papa bought her a pair of new trousers, but it couldn't be worn as it shrank in the wash. Her mother got angry.

2 But Jenny said. “Mama, I can wear it if you have me a bath.”

## 生词宝库

papa [pəˈpɑː] *n.* < 口 > 爸爸

trousers [ˈtraʊzəz] *n.* 裤子

shrank [ʃræŋk] *v.* 缩水（动词 shrink 的过去式）

angry [ˈæŋgrɪ] *adj.* 生气的

wear [weə] *v.* 穿

bath [bɑːθ] *n.* 洗澡

# Our Ancestors Survive

# 祖先的生存

1 Two boys are talking with each other.

2 "You see, in the old times there were no electricity, no radios, no televisions. How could our ancestors survive?"

3 "So they all died."

## 点睛译文

1 两个孩子正在交谈。

2 “你想，古代没有电，没有收音机，也没有电视。我们的祖先怎么活得了呢？”

3 “所以他们都死了。”

## 生词宝库

electricity [ɪˌlekˈtrɪsətɪ] *n.* 电

radio [ˈreɪdɪəʊ] *n.* 收音机

ancestor [ˈænsestə] *n.* 祖宗

survive [səˈvaɪv] *v.* 存活

# Hen's Legs

# 母鸡的腿

爆笑故事

1 Son: Why are the hen's legs so short?

2 Dad: You are a fool. If the hen's legs were too long, wouldn't they drop their eggs into pieces when laying?

点睛译文

1 儿子：为什么母鸡的腿那么短？

2 父亲：你真笨。如果母鸡的腿很长，它们下蛋时，鸡蛋不就都摔破了吗？

生词宝库

leg [leg] *n.* 腿

short [ʃɔːt] *adj.* 短的

fool [fuːl] *n.* 傻瓜

long [lɒŋ] *adj.* 长的

drop [drɒp] *v.* 使落下

# The Movie Ticket
# 电影票

1 “How much is the movie ticket?”

2 “Ten kops, kid.”

3 “I only have five kops. Please let me in. I’ll see it only with one eye.”

1 “电影票多少钱一张？”

2 “10 戈比，孩子。”

3 “我只有 5 戈比。请让我进去吧。我只用一只眼睛看。”

生词宝库

movie [ˈmuːvɪ] *n.* 电影

ticket [ˈtɪkɪt] *n.* 票

kop [ˈkəup] *n.* 戈比（苏联小铜板，即 kopeck）

# Change from Monkeys

# 猴子变的

## 点睛译文

1 “妈妈，人是从猴子变过来的吗？”

2 “是的。”

3 “噢，难怪猴子越来越少了。”

## 爆笑故事

1 “Mama, do people change from monkeys?”

2 “Yeah.”

3 “Oh, no wonder monkeys are getting fewer and fewer.”

## 生词宝库

change [tʃeɪndʒ] *v.* 变成

monkey [ˈmʌŋkɪ] *n.* 猴子

wonder [ˈwʌndə] *n.* 惊奇

fewer [ˈfjuːə] *adj.* 少的

# The Timid Sun
# 胆小的太阳

爆笑故事

1 Younger Brother: How timid the sun is!

2 Elder Brother: Why do you think so?

3 Younger Brother: Because it only dares to come out in the daytime.

点睛译文

1 弟弟：太阳多么胆小！

2 哥哥：你为什么这样想？

3 弟弟：因为它只有白天才敢出来。

生词宝库

timid ['tɪmɪd] *adj.* 胆怯的
elder ['eldə] *adj.* 年龄较大的
dare [deə] *v.* 胆敢
daytime ['deɪtaɪm] *n.* 白天

# What Do I Get
# 我能得到什么

## 点睛译文

1 老师：如果我把一块牛排对半切后再对半切，我能得到几块儿？

2 汤米：4块。

3 老师：那我要是再切两次呢？

4 汤米：能得到汉堡。

## 爆笑故事

1 Teacher: If I cut a beefsteak in half and then cut the half in half, what do I get?

2 Tommy: Quarters.

3 Teacher: And then if I cut it twice again?

4 Tommy: Hamburger.

## 生词宝库

beefsteak [ˈbiːfsteɪk] *n.* 牛排

quarter [ˈkwɔːtə] *n.* 四分之一

hamburger [ˈhæmbɜːgə] *n.* 汉堡包

# Where's the Father

# 父亲在哪

## 爆笑故事

1 Two brothers were looking at some beautiful paintings.

2 "Look," said the elder brother. "How nice these paintings are!"

3 "Yes," said the younger, "but in all these paintings there is only the mother and the children. Where is the father?"

4 The elder brother thought for a moment and then explained, "Obviously he was painting the pictures."

## 点睛译文

1 兄弟俩在看一些漂亮的绘画。

2 "看，" 哥哥说，"这些画多漂亮呀！"

3 "是啊，" 弟弟说道，"可是所有的这些画中都只有妈妈和孩子。那爸爸去哪儿了呢？"

4 哥哥想了一会儿，然后解释道："很明显，他当时正在画这些画呗。"

## 生词宝库

beautiful [ˈbjuːtɪfʊl] *adj.* 美丽的；漂亮的

painting [ˈpeɪntɪŋ] *n.* 绘画

moment [ˈməʊmənt] *n.* 片刻

paint [peɪnt] *v.* 绘画

# A Girl's Wish
# 小女孩的愿望

## 点睛译文

1 在观看完芭蕾舞表演回家的路上，幼儿园老师问学生的观后感。班上最小的女孩说，她希望舞蹈演员可以长得更高一点儿，那么他们就不用整天踮着脚尖了。

## 爆笑故事

1 On the way home after watching a ballet performance, the kindergarten teacher asked her students what they thought of it. The smallest girl in the class said she wished the dancers were taller so that they would not have to stand on their toes all the time.

## 生词宝库

ballet [ˈbæleɪ] *n.* 芭蕾舞
performance [pəˈfɔːməns] *n.* 表演
kindergarten [ˈkɪndəgɑːtn] *n.* 幼儿园
dancer [ˈdɑːnsə] *n.* 跳舞者
toe [təʊ] *n.* 脚趾

# I Want a Nightmare
# 想做坏梦

## 爆笑故事

1 Before the final examination, Tom told his mother, "Mom, I had a dream last night that I'd passed today's exam."

2 "Don't trust dreams, dear. It is said what you experience in dreams usually turns out to be the opposite." Mother replied.

3 "Then I do hope I'll fail the other subjects in my dream tonight." Tom said.

## 点睛译文

1 在期末考试之前，汤姆告诉他的母亲："妈妈，我昨天晚上做了一个梦，梦见我通过了今天的考试。"

2 "不要相信梦，亲爱的。据说梦中的经历通常与现实相反。"妈妈答道。

3 "那么，我真希望在今晚的梦中，我其他的功课都不及格。"汤姆说。

## 生词宝库

final [ˈfaɪnəl] *adj.* 最终的

trust [trʌst] *v.* 信任

dream [driːm] *n.* 梦

experience [ɪkˈspɪərɪəns] *v.* 经历

opposite [ˈɒpəzɪt] *adj.* 相反的

subject [ˈsʌbdʒɪkt] *n.* 科目

# It's Part of the Game
# 这是游戏的一部分

1 妈妈：玛丽，你为什么这样大喊大叫的？为什么不能像埃迪那样安安静静地玩儿呢？你看埃迪一声儿都不出。

2 玛丽：妈妈，埃迪当然不会出声了，因为我们俩正在玩爸爸回家迟到的游戏呢，他扮演爸爸，我扮演你。

1 Mother: Mary, why do you yell and scream so much? Play quietly like Eddie. See, he doesn't make a sound.

2 Mary: Of course he doesn't. Mom, it's part of the game we are playing. He is Daddy coming home late, and I'm you.

yell [jel] *v.* 大叫

scream [skriːm] *v.* 尖叫

sound [saʊnd] *n.* 声音

game [geɪm] *n.* 游戏

# I Taught the Teacher

# 我教老师

1 Mother asked her little boy: "Darling, what did the teacher teach you today?"

2 "Nothing, Mum." answered the son proudly, "instead, she asked me how much one plus two was, and I told her three."

点睛译文

1 母亲问她年幼的儿子："宝贝，今天老师教了你些什么？"

2 儿子骄傲地说："什么都没教，妈妈。她反倒问我1加2等于几，我告诉她等于3。"

词汇无障碍

proudly [ˈpraʊdlɪ] *adv.* 得意洋洋地

instead [ɪnˈsted] *adv.* 代替

plus [plʌs] prep. 加，加上

tell [tel] *v.* 告诉

# A Small Boy and a Donkey
# 小男孩与驴子

1 一个小男孩牵着头驴子穿过部队营房。

2 几名士兵想跟小家伙开个玩笑。一名士兵问："小孩，你把你哥哥牵得这么紧干什么？"

3 "这样，他就不会去参军了。"小家伙眼都不眨地回答道。

1 A small boy leading a donkey passed by an Army camp.

2 A couple of soldiers wanted to have some fun with the lad. "What are you holding onto your brother so tight for, sonny?" asked one of them.

3 "So he won't join the army." the youngster replied without blinking an eye.

## 生词宝库

donkey [ˈdɒŋkɪ] *n.* 驴
camp [kæmp] *n.* 营地
lad [læd] *n.* 少年，小伙子
tight [taɪt] *adj.* 紧的
blink [blɪŋk] *v.* 眨眼

# The Woman Who Loves You Most 最爱你的女人

1 One evening I drove my husband's car to the shopping mall.

2 On my return, I noticed that how dusty the outside of his car was and cleaned it up a bit. When I finally entered the house, I called out: "The woman who loves you the most in the world just cleaned your headlights and windshield."

3 My husband looked up and said: "Mom's here?"

1 一天晚上我开着丈夫的车去购物。

2 回来后我发现车身沾满了灰尘，于是擦洗了一阵。当我最后走进屋里时大声喊："世界上最爱你的女人刚擦洗了你的车灯和挡风玻璃。"

3 我丈夫抬头看了看，说："妈妈来了？"

## 生词宝库

mall [mɔːl] *n.* 购物中心
return [rɪˈtɜːn] *n.* 返回
dusty [ˈdʌstɪ] *adj.* 落满灰尘的
enter [ˈentə] *v.* 进入
headlight [ˈhedlaɪt] *n.* 前灯
windshield [ˈwɪndʃiːld] *n.* 挡风玻璃

# Fried Chicken
# 炸鸡

## 点睛译文

1 老师在课堂上向学生们展示了各种各样的鸟的图片。然后他问其中一名学生：“杰克，你最喜欢哪种鸟儿啊？”

2 杰克想了想，回答：“炸鸡，老师。”

## 爆笑故事

1 In class the teacher showed pictures of various birds. Then he asked one of the students, “What kind of bird do you like best, Jack?”

2 Jack thought for a moment, and then answered, “Fried chicken, sir.”

## 生词宝库

show [ʃəʊ] *v.* 展示

various [ˈveərɪəs] *adj.* 各种各样的

kind [kaɪnd] *n.* 种类

bird [bɜːd] *n.* 鸟

fried [fraɪd] *adj.* 炸过的

chicken [ˈtʃɪkɪn] *n.* 鸡肉

# I've Just Bitten My Tongue

# 我刚咬破自己的舌头

1 "Are we poisonous?" the young snake asked his mother.

2 "Yes, dear." she replied, "Why do you ask?"

3 "Cause I've just bitten my tongue!"

1 "我们有毒吗？"一条年幼的蛇问它的母亲。

2 "是的，亲爱的，"她回答说，"你问这个干什么？"

3 "因为我刚刚咬破自己的舌头了。"

## 生词宝库

poisonous [ˈpɔɪzənəs] *adj.* 有毒的

snake [sneɪk] *n.* 蛇

tongue [tʌŋ] *n.* 舌头

# He's Just Been to the Zoo
# 他刚去过动物园

1 当我在银行里排队时，发现一位妇女抱着一个小孩站在一个窗口前。男孩正在吃一个面包卷，并将面包卷戳向出纳员，出纳员笑着摇了摇头。

2 “别这样，亲爱的。”男孩的妈妈说。然后她转向出纳员说：“对不起，小伙子。请原谅我的儿子，他刚去过动物园。”

1 When I was waiting in line at the bank, I noticed a woman holding a small child at one of the windows. The boy was eating a roll, which he thrust at the teller. The teller smiled and shook his head.

2 “No, no, dear.” said the boy's mom. And then turning to the teller, she said, “I beg your pardon, young man. Please forgive my son. He's just been to the zoo.”

生词宝库

line [laɪn] *n.* 排

thrust [θrʌst] *v.* 戳

teller [ˈtelə] *n.* <美> 出纳员

pardon [ˈpɑːdən] *n.* 原谅

# How to Be Like a Gentleman
# 怎样做一名绅士

1 Dick was seven years old, and his sister, Catherine, was five. One day their mother took them to their aunt's house to play while she went to the big city to buy some new clothes.

2 The children played for an hour, and then at half past four their aunt took Dick into the kitchen. She gave him a nice cake and a knife and said to him, "Now here's a knife, Dick. Cut this cake in half and give one of the pieces to your sister, but remember to do it like a gentleman."

3 "Like a gentleman?" Dick asked. "How do gentlemen do it?"

4 "They always give the bigger piece to the other person." answered his aunt at once.

5 "Oh." said Dick.

6 He thought about this for a few seconds. Then he took the cake to his sister and said to her, "Cut this cake in half, Catherine."

## 点睛译文

1 迪克7岁，他的妹妹凯瑟琳5岁。一天，妈妈把他们带到姨妈家去玩，自己就到大城市去买些新的衣服。

2 孩子们玩了个把小时，在4点半的时候，姨妈领着迪克走进了厨房。她交给迪克一块精美的蛋糕和一把刀子，并对他说："喏，迪克，给你刀子，把这块蛋糕切成两块，给你妹妹一块。不过，你得记住，要做得像个绅士那样。"

3 迪克问："像一个绅士？绅士怎样做呢？"

4 他姨妈马上回答说："绅士总是把大的一块让给别人。"

5 迪克说了一声"噢"。

6 他对此想了一会，然后，他把蛋糕拿给妹妹，并对她说："凯瑟琳，你来把这块蛋糕切成两块吧。"

aunt [ɑːnt] *n.* 姨妈

cake [keɪk] *n.* 蛋糕

knife [naɪf] *n.* 刀

half [hɑːf] *n.* 一半

gentleman [ˈdʒentlmən] *n.* 绅士

# Son and Dad
# 儿子和爸爸

1 Son: Dad, are you available on Friday afternoon?

2 Dad: What ah?

3 Son: The school will hold a mini-parents forum!

4 Dad: What is mini-parents forum?

5 Son: Only my teacher, you and I will participate in it!

## 点睛译文

1 儿子：爸爸，星期五下午您有空吗？

2 爸爸：什么事啊？

3 儿子：学校要开微型家长座谈会！

4 爸爸：什么叫微型家长座谈会？

5 儿子：就是只有班主任，你和我参加！

## 生词宝库

available [ə'veɪləbl] *adj.* 有空的

mini ['mɪnɪ] *adj.* 微型的

forum ['fɔːrəm] *n.* 座谈会

participate [pɑː'tɪsɪpeɪt] *v.* 参加

# A Girl like Your Mother
# 像母亲一样的女孩

1 无论带哪一个女孩回家，这个青年人总会遭到母亲的反对。

2 一位朋友劝他说："找一个像你母亲一样的女孩——那你母亲一定会喜欢她。"

3 于是这个青年人不停地找啊找，终于找到了这么个女孩。他跟给了他意见的那位朋友说："正像你说的那样，我找到一个长相、谈吐、穿着打扮，甚至连烹饪都和我母亲一样的女孩。也正像你说的那样，我母亲喜欢她。"

4 "那后来呢？"朋友问。

5 "什么也没发生。"青年人说，"我父亲讨厌她！"

1 No matter which girl he brought home, the young man found disapproval from his mother.

2 A friend gave him advice, "Find a girl just like your mother — then she's bound to like her."

3 So the young man searched constantly, and finally found the girl. He told his friendly adviser, "Just like you said, I found a girl who looks, talks, dresses, and even cooks like my mother. And just as you said, mother likes her."

4 "So," asked the friend, "what happened?"

5 "Nothing." said the young man, "My father hates her!"

生词宝库

disapproval [ˌdɪsəˈpruːvl] *n.* 不赞成
advice [ədˈvaɪs] *n.* 建议
constantly [ˈkɒnstəntlɪ] *adv.* 不断地
adviser [ədˈvaɪzə] *n.* 劝告者
dress [dres] *v.* 打扮
hate [heɪt] *v.* 憎恨

# An Exact Number
# 精确数字

## 爆笑故事

1 A tourist was visiting New Mexico and was amazed at the dinosaur bones lying about.

2 "How old are these bones?" the tourist asked an elderly Native American, who served as a guide.

3 "Exactly one hundred million and three years old."

4 "How can you be so sure?" inquired the tourist.

5 "Well," replied the guide, "a geologist came by here and told me these bones were one hundred million years old, and that was exactly three years ago."

## 点睛译文

1 一位游客在新墨西哥游览，他对随处可见的恐龙化石甚感惊奇。

2 "这些化石有多久的历史？"游客问一个上了年纪的印第安人。他是游客的向导。

3 "整整10亿零3年了。"

4 "你怎么这么肯定？"游客问道。

5 "哦，"向导回答道，"一个地质学家来过这儿，他告诉我说这些化石有10亿年了，再加上那是整整3年前的事了。"

## 生词宝库

tourist [ˈtʊərɪst] *n.* 旅游者

amazed [əˈmeɪzd] *adj.* 吃惊的

dinosaur [ˈdaɪnəsɔː] *n.* 恐龙

bone [bəʊn] *n.* 骨

native [ˈneɪtɪv] *adj.* 本国的；当地的

guide [gaɪd] *n.* 向导

geologist [dʒɪˈɒlədʒɪst] *n.* 地质学家

# My Wife Barks
# 汪汪叫的妻子

## 点睛译文

1 一个结婚10年的男人正在请教一位婚姻顾问。

2 "刚结婚那会儿，我非常幸福。我在店里操劳一整天回到家，我的小狗会绕着我跑，汪汪叫，而我的妻子会给我拿来拖鞋。现在一切都变了。我回到家里，我的狗给我拿来拖鞋，我的妻子对着我汪汪叫。"

3 "我不知道你在抱怨什么，"婚姻顾问说，"你得到的服务还是一样的呀。"

## 爆笑故事

1 A man who had been married for ten years was consulting a marriage counselor.

2 "When I was first married, I was very happy. I'd come home from a hard day down at the shop, and my little dog would race around barking, and my wife would bring me my slippers. Now everything's changed. When I come home, my dog brings me my slippers, and my wife barks at me."

3 "I don't know what you're complaining about," said the counselor, "You're still getting the same service."

## 生词宝库

consult [kən'sʌlt] *v.* 请教
marriage ['mærɪdʒ] *n.* 结婚；婚姻
counselor ['kaʊnsələ] *n.* 顾问
bark [bɑːk] *v.*（狗）吠
slipper ['slɪpə] *n.* 拖鞋
service ['sɜːvɪs] *n.* 服务

# A Speeding Motorist

# 超速的司机

## 爆笑故事

1 A highway patrol officer stopped a speeding motorist. "Don't you know what the blinking lights and siren mean?" he demanded.

2 "Yes, sir." replied the driver.

3 "Then why didn't you pull over immediately?"

4 "I would have, officer." the man said. "But last month my wife ran off with a policeman, and I was afraid you were bringing her back."

## 点睛译文

1 一位公路巡警截住了一个超速的司机。"难道你不知道闪烁灯和警笛的意思吗？"他责问道。

2 "知道，长官。"司机回答说。

3 "那你为什么不立即靠边停车？"

4 "我本来想这样做的，长官。"那男子回答说，"但上个月我妻子和一位警察私奔了，我是害怕你把她带回来。"

## 生词宝库

highway [ˈhaɪweɪ] *n.* 公路

patrol [pəˈtrəʊl] *n.* 巡逻

motorist [ˈməʊtərɪst] *n.* 驾车的人

siren [ˈsaɪrən] *n.* 汽笛

pull over 路边停车

# The New Baby
# 新生儿

1 泰勒夫妇有一个7岁的男孩，名叫帕特。现在泰勒太太正怀着第二胎。帕特在别人家看见过婴儿，他不太喜欢他们，所以他对自己家里也将有一个婴儿的消息感到不满。

2 一天晚上，泰勒夫妇正在为这个婴儿的降生做计划。泰勒先生说：“有了婴儿，我们的房子就会变得太小，不够住了。”

3 帕特恰好在这个时候走进屋，他问：“你们在说什么？”

4 他的母亲回答说：“我们在说我们现在得搬家，因为婴儿就要出生了。”

5 “那没用，”帕特绝望地说，“他会跟我们到那儿去的。”

1 Mr. and Mrs. Taylor had a seven year old boy named Pat. Now Mrs. Taylor was expecting another child. Pat had seen babies in other people's houses and had not liked them very much, so he was not delighted about the news that there was soon going to be one in his house too.

2 One evening Mr. and Mrs. Taylor were making plans for the baby's arrival. “This house won't be big enough for us all when the baby comes.” said Mr. Taylor.”

3 Pat came into the room just then and said, “What are you talking about”

4 “We were saying that we'll have to move to another house now, because the new baby's coming.” his mother answered.

5 “It's no use,” said Pat hopelessly, “He'll follow us there.”

## 生词宝库

expect [ɪkˈspekt] *v.* 期待

house [haʊs] *n.* 家庭

delighted [dɪˈlaɪtɪd] *adj.* 高兴的

plan [plæn] *n.* 计划

arrival [əˈraɪvəl] *n.* 到来

hopelessly [ˈhəʊpləslɪ] *adv.* 绝望地

follow [ˈfɒləʊ] *v.* 跟随

# Three Turtles
# 三只乌龟

## 点睛译文

1 三只乌龟决定去喝咖啡。它们刚到咖啡店的门口，就下起雨来。

2 于是最大的那只乌龟对最小的乌龟说:“回家去取伞吧。”

3 最小的乌龟说:“如果你们不喝我的咖啡，我就去。”

4 “我们不喝。”另外两只乌龟答应说。

5 两年后，大乌龟对中乌龟说:“好吧，我猜他肯定不回来了，我们可以把它的咖啡喝掉了。”

6 正在这时，一个声音从门外传来:“你们要是喝了，我就不去。”

## 爆笑故事

1 Three turtles decided to have a cup of coffee. Just as they got into the cafe, it started to rain.

2 The biggest turtle said to the smallest one, “Go home and get the umbrella.”

3 The little turtle replied, “I will, if you don't drink my coffee.”

4 “We won't.” the other two promised.

5 Two years later the big turtle said to the middle turtle, “Well, I guess he isn't coming back, so we might as well drink his coffee.”

6 Just then a voice called from outside the door, “If you do, I won't go.”

## 生词宝库

turtle [ˈtɜːtl] *n.* 龟

umbrella [ʌmˈbrelə] *n.* 伞

promise [ˈprɒmɪs] *v.* 答应

voice [vɔɪs] *n.* 声音

# An Exceptional Phenomenon 罕见

1 4-year-old Begin and his cousin scrambled for toys.

2 His mum told him: “You are older brother because you’re older than your (cousin) sister. You should give ground to her.”

3 Begin thought a little but maintained, “My sister must give ground to me when she grows older than I.”

4 His uncle around overheard and said: “Such a thing hardly occurs.”

## 点睛译文

1 4岁的贝让和小妹妹争玩具。

2 妈妈对他说：“你大，你是哥哥，要让着小妹妹点儿。”

3 贝让想了想，坚持说：“等妹妹长得比我大了，她也得让着我。”

4 姨夫在一旁听了说：“这种情况相当罕见。”

## 生词宝库

scramble [ˈscræmbl] v. 争夺

give ground 退却；让步

maintain [meɪnˈteɪn] v. 坚持；坚守

overhear [ˌəuvəˈhɪə] v. 听见

occur [əˈkɜː] v. 发生

# I and Boss
# 我和老板

1 When I take a long time, I am slow. When my boss takes a long time, he is thorough.

2 When I don't do it, I am lazy. When my boss doesn't do it, he is too busy.

3 When I do something without being told, I am trying to be smart. When my boss does the same, that is initiative.

4 When I please my boss, I am ass-kissing. When my boss pleases his boss, he is co-operating.

5 When I do well, my boss never remembers. When I do wrong, he never forgets.

1 我做事情花了长时间，是效率低；老板做事情花了长时间，是深思熟虑。

2 我没有做完事情，是懒惰；老板没有做完事情，是太繁忙。

3 没有人要求我做的事情我做了，是自作聪明；老板做了同样的事情，是首创。

4 我取悦老板，是献媚；老板取悦他的老板，是合作。

5 我干得好，老板从来不会想起；我干得不好，老板从来不会忘记。

## 生词宝库

boss [bɒs] *n.* 老板

thorough [ˈθʌrə] *adj.* 彻底的，细致的

lazy [ˈleɪzɪ] *adj.* 懒惰的

busy [ˈbɪzɪ] *adj.* 忙碌的

initiative [ɪˈnɪʃətɪv] *adj.* 创始的

ass-kissing [ˈæsˈkɪsɪŋ] *n.* 溜须拍马

co-operate [kəʊˈɒpəreɪt] *v.* 合作

# Bring Me a Glass of Milk

# 捎杯牛奶

## 爆笑故事

1 At 2 a.m, Mrs. Culkin was convinced that she had heard a prowler in the living room. "Tiptoe down-stairs." she told her husband, "Don't turn on the lights. Sneak up him before he knows what's happening."

2 Dutifully Mr. Culkin put on his robe. Just as he reached the bedroom door, his wife added, "And when you come back, bring me a glass of milk."

## 点睛译文

1 半夜两点，卡尔金太太确信听到客厅有贼，便对丈夫说："别开灯，轻手轻脚地下楼，别让贼发觉，悄悄靠近他。"

2 卡尔金先生披上外套，责无旁贷地去捉贼。刚走到卧室门口，他妻子又补充说："回来时给我捎杯牛奶。"

## 生词宝库

convince [kən'vɪns] *v.* 使确信

prowler ['praʊlə] *n.* 小偷

tiptoe ['tɪptəʊ] *v.* 蹑手蹑脚地走

light [laɪt] *n.* 灯

dutifully ['dju:tɪfʊlɪ] *adv.* 忠实地

robe [rəʊb] *n.* 睡袍

milk [mɪlk] *n.* 牛奶

# Way of Inducing
# 招客有方

1 在洗衣店，我看到招牌上写着：“上午 10 点（送）进，下午 5 点（取）出”。因此我就告诉店主我想在下午 5 点取衣。

2 “下午 5 点还不能取，”他说。

3 “但是你的牌子上写着：‘上午 10 点进，下午 5 点出’。”我提醒他说。

4 “哦，”他回答说，“那指的是我。”

1 At the cleaners, I noticed the sign saying “In by 10 a.m., out by 5 p.m.”. So I told the owner that I wanted to pick my clothing up at five.

2 “It won’t be ready.” he said.

3 “But your sign says, ‘In by 10 a.m., out by 5 p.m.’.” I reminded him.

4 “Oh,” he replied, “that means me.”

## 生词宝库

cleaners [ˈkliːnə] *n.* 干洗店
sign [saɪn] *n.* 指示牌
owner [ˈəʊnə] *n.* 老板
pick [pɪk] *v.* 取
ready [ˈredɪ] *adj.* 准备好
mean [miːn] *v.* 意思是

# How Could Anyone Stoop so Low
# 哪有人能弯腰弯那么低的

## 爆笑故事

1 Our manager at the restaurant where I worked was a much beloved, jovial man. But there was one subject you didn't dare discuss in front of him — his height. Or, should I say, he's lack of it.

2 One day, he stormed through the door and announced angrily, "Someone just picked my pocket!"

3 Most of my fellow waitresses and I were speechless, except for the one who blurted out, "How could anyone stoop so low?

## 点睛译文

1 我们的餐厅经理是一位深受大家爱戴、和蔼而又快乐的人。但在他面前有一件事不能提——他的身高。或者，我应该说，他是有点矮！

2 一天，经理怒气冲冲地撞门而入，高声说："有人拿了我的钱包！"

3 我和其她大部分女招待都没敢吱声，但有人却蹦出一句话："哪有人能弯腰弯那么低的啊！"

## 生词宝库

manager [ˈmænɪdʒə] *n.* 经理
restaurant [ˈrestrɒnt] *n.* 餐馆
jovial [ˈdʒəʊvɪəl] *adj.* 快活的
height [haɪt] *n.* 身高
lack [læk] *v.* 缺乏
announce [əˈnaʊns] *v.* 说；声称
waitress [ˈweɪtrɪs] *n.* 女服务员
speechless [ˈspiːtʃlɪs] *adj.* 说不出话的
blurt [blɜːt] *v.* 未加思索地冲口说出
stoop [stuːp] *v.* 弯腰

# Where It Should Be Plugged 应该要插在哪

## 点睛译文

1 一位母亲十分善于利用每一个机会对孩子进行教育。她的儿子只有3岁。一天，她拿着一个插头对儿子说："看，这里有两个铜片，那它一定要插在有两个孔的地方。你说它应该插在哪儿呢？"母亲期待着儿子的回答。

2 "插在鼻子里！"儿子回答说。

## 爆笑故事

1 A mother is very good at using every chance to educate his son, who was only three years old. One day, she took a plug and said to her son, "Look, there are two pieces of copper, so it must be plugged in a place where there are two holes. Where do you think it should be plugged?" She waited for an answer expectedly.

2 "Plug in nose is the answer." The son says.

## 生词宝库

chance [tʃɑːns] *n.* 机会

educate [ˈedjuːkeɪt] *v.* 教育

plug [plʌg] *n.* 插头；*v.* 插入

copper [ˈkɒpə] *n.* 铜

hole [həʊl] *n.* 洞，孔

# What Was It She Wanted

# 她想要买什么

1 A store manager heard a clerk tell a customer, "No, ma'am, we haven't had any for a while, and it doesn't look as if we'll be getting soon."

2 Horrified, the manager came running over to the customer and said, "Of course, we'll have some soon; we placed an order last week."

3 Then the manager drew the clerk aside: "Never, never, never say we are out of anything — say we've got it on order and it's coming. Now what was it she wanted?"

4 "Rain." said the clerk.

1 一个商店经理听见一个店员对顾客说："不，夫人，这会儿没有，一时半会儿看来也不会有。"

2 经理惊恐万分地跑到顾客跟前说："当然，马上就会有的。我们上周订了货。"

3 然后经理把店员拉到一边："千万，千万，千万不要说我们没有什么——说我们已经订了货，货马上就到。现在你说她要买什么？"

4 "雨。"店员说。

## 生词宝库

clerk [klɑːk] *n.* 职员

customer ['kʌstəmə] *n.* 顾客

horrified ['hɒrɪfaɪd] *adj.*（表现出）恐惧的

order ['ɔːdə] *n.* 订单

# A Preacher Is Buying a Parrot 传教士买鹦鹉

1 一个传教士在买鹦鹉。“你确信它不会大喊大叫或咒骂别人吗？”传教士问。

2 “哦，绝对不会。它是一只虔诚的鹦鹉。”店主保证说。

3 “你看见它腿上的这些细绳了吗？当你拉动右边的这根，它会背诵天主经；当你拉动左边的那根，它会背诵赞美诗。”

4 “太棒了！”传教士说，“但是如果我同时拉动两边绳子，会发生什么呢？”

5 “我会从树干上掉下去的，你这个笨蛋！”鹦鹉尖声说道。

## 爆笑故事

1 A preacher is buying a parrot. “Are you sure it doesn’t scream, yell, or swear?” asked the preacher.

2 “Oh absolutely. It’s a religious parrot.” the storekeeper assures him.

3 “Do you see those strings on his legs? When you pull the right one, he recites the Lord’s Prayer, and when you pull the left he recites the 23rd Psalm.”

4 “Wonderful!” says the preacher, “But what happens if you pull both strings?”

5 “I fall off my perch, you stupid fool!” Screeched the parrot.

## 生词宝库

parrot [ˈpærət] *n.* 鹦鹉

swear [sweə] *v.* 咒骂

religious [rɪˈlɪdʒəs] *adj.* 虔诚的

storekeeper [ˈstɔːkiːpə] *n.* 零售店店主

string [strɪŋ] *n.* 线

recite [rɪˈsaɪt] *v.* 背诵

perch [pɜːtʃ] *n.* 杆

screech [skriːtʃ] *v.* 尖声叫

# Dog Can't Read
# 狗不识字

## 爆笑故事

1 Mrs. Brown: Oh, my dear, I have lost my precious little dog!

2 Mrs. Smith: But you must put an advertisement in the papers!

3 Mrs. Brown: It's no use; my little dog can't read.

## 点睛译文

1 布朗夫人：哦，亲爱的，我把心爱的小狗给丢了！

2 史密斯夫人：可是你该在报纸上登广告啊！

3 布朗夫人：没有用的，我的小狗不认识字。

## 生词宝库

precious [ˈpreʃəs] *adj.* 珍爱的

advertisement [ədˈvɜːtɪsmənt] *n.* 广告

read [riːd] *v.* 理解，读懂

# Diner Is Ready

# 晚饭好了

1 我的烧饭手艺向来是家人嘲笑的对象。

2 一天晚上，晚餐我准备得有点儿太快了，厨房里满是烟，结果烟雾探查器报起警来。尽管我的两个孩子都在学校里接受过防火安全训练，可是他们并没有对报警声作出反应。我感到很恼火，满幢房子乱冲去寻找他们。

3 我在洗澡间找到他们，发现他们正在洗手。我的声音盖过了烟雾警报的嗡嗡声，我叫他们辨别那声音。

4 “是烟雾探查器。”他们异口同声地说。

5 “你们知道那声音意味着什么吗？”我责问道。

6 “当然，”我的大孩子回答道，“晚饭准备好了。”

1 My cooking has always been the target of family jokes.

2 One evening, as I prepared dinner a bit too quickly, the kitchen filled with smoke and the smoke detector went off. Although both of my children had received fire-safety training at school, they did not respond to the alarm. Annoyed, I stormed through the house in search of them.

3 I found them in the bathroom, washing their hands. Over the loud buzzing of the smoke alarm, I asked them to identify the sound.

4 “It’s the smoke detector.” they replied in unison.

5 “Do you know what that sound means?” I demanded.

6 “Sure,” my older replied, “Dinner’s ready.”

## 生词宝库

cooking [ˈkʊkɪŋ] *n.* 烹饪
target [ˈtɑːgɪt] *n.* 目标
prepare [prɪˈpeə] *v.* 准备
detector [dɪˈtektə] *n.* 探测器
receive [rɪˈsiːv] *v.* 接受
respond [rɪˈsiːv] *v.* 作出反应
annoyed [əˈnɔɪd] *adj.* 恼怒的
storm [stɔːm] *v.* 横冲直撞
buzzing [ˈbʌzɪŋ] *n.* 嗡嗡声
identify [aɪˈdentɪfaɪ] *v.* 辨认出

# Goodbye, Money

# 再见，美元

## 爆笑故事

1 On a trip to Disney World in Florida, my husband and I and our two children devoted ourselves wholeheartedly to the wonders of this attraction. After three exhausting days, we headed for home.

2 As we drove away, our son waved and said, "Goodbye, Mickey."

3 Our daughter waved and said, "Goodbye, Minnie."

4 My husband waved, rather weakly, and said, "Goodbye, Money."

## 点睛译文

1 弗罗里达州的迪斯尼乐园是一个迷人的地方。一次我和丈夫以及两个孩子前往旅游，我们全身心地沉醉在它的各种奇观之中。精疲力竭地玩了3天之后，我们要回家了。

2 当我们驱车离开时，儿子挥手说："再见，米奇。"

3 女儿挥着手说："再见，米妮。"

4 丈夫也有气无力地挥了挥手，说道："再见，米元（美元）。"

## 生词宝库

trip [trɪp] *n.* 旅行

devote [dɪˈvəʊt] *v.* 集中

wholeheartedly [ˌhəʊlˈhɑːtɪdlɪ] *adv.* 全心全意地

attraction [əˈtrækʃn] *n.* 吸引

exhausting [ɪgˈzɔːstɪŋ] *adj.* 疲倦的；筋疲力尽的

weakly [ˈwiːklɪ] *adv.* 虚弱地

# A Blind Beggar

# 盲人乞丐

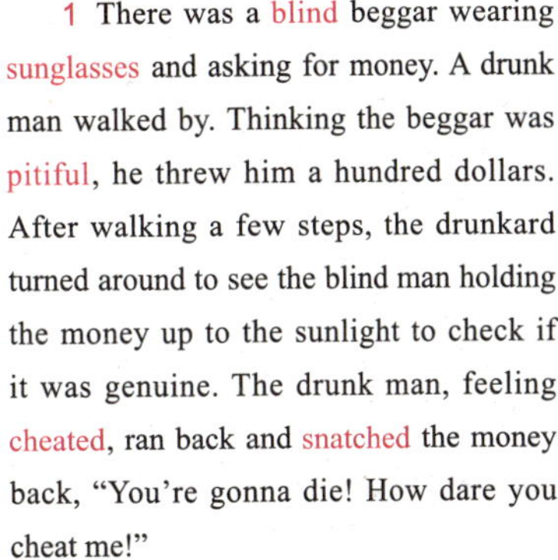

## 爆笑故事

1 There was a blind beggar wearing sunglasses and asking for money. A drunk man walked by. Thinking the beggar was pitiful, he threw him a hundred dollars. After walking a few steps, the drunkard turned around to see the blind man holding the money up to the sunlight to check if it was genuine. The drunk man, feeling cheated, ran back and snatched the money back, "You're gonna die! How dare you cheat me!"

2 The blind man, not wanting to feel like a cheater, retorted, "Hey man, I'm sorry, I'm just here to replace my friend who really is blind. He went to the bathroom, and should be right back... Actually... I'm mute."

3 "Oh, oh, in that case..." whereupon the drunk threw the money back and stumbled away.

## 点睛译文

1 一个盲人乞丐戴着墨镜在街上行乞。一个醉汉走过来，觉得他可怜，就扔了一百元给他。走了一段路，醉汉一回头，恰好看见那个盲人正对着太阳分辨那张百元大钞的真假。醉汉觉得被欺骗了，过来一把夺回钱道："你不想活了，竟敢骗老子！"

2 盲人乞丐一脸委屈地说："嘿，大哥，真对不起啊，我是替一个朋友在这儿看一下，他是个瞎子，去上厕所了，马上就回来……其实……我是个哑巴。"

3 "哦，哦，是这样子啊……"于是醉汉扔下钱，又摇摇晃晃地走了。

## 生词宝库

blind [blaɪnd] *adj.* 瞎的

sunglass [ˈsʌnglɑːs] *n.* 太阳眼镜

pitiful [ˈpɪtɪfl] *adj.* 可怜的

cheat [tʃiːt] *v.* 欺骗

snatch [snætʃ] *v.* 抢走

retort [rɪˈtɔːt] *v.* 反驳

mute [mjuːt] *adj.* 哑的

stumble [ˈstʌmbəl] *v.* 蹒跚

# How Do I Get the Gum Out
# 怎么把口香糖取出来呢

## 爆笑故事

1 Distributing chewing gum to the passengers, the stewardess explained it was used to keep their ears from popping.

2 When the plane landed, one of the passengers rushed up to her and said, "I'm meeting my wife right away. How do I get the gum out from my ears?"

## 点睛译文

1 当空姐给乘客们发口香糖的时候，她解释说口香糖有助于他们防止耳鸣。

2 飞机着陆后，一位乘客跑到这位空姐面前，说道："我马上就要见到我妻子了。我怎么才能把口香糖从耳朵里面取出来呢？"

## 生词宝库

distribute [dɪˈstrɪbjuːt] v. 分配
stewardess [ˌstjuːəˈdes] n. 女乘务员
pop [ˈpɒp] v. 砰砰地响
land [lænd] v. 登陆；着陆
rush [rʌʃ] v. 冲；奔

# Did Your Father Help You

# 你爸爸帮你了吗

## 点睛译文

1 一天，蒂姆的数学老师看了他的作业，发现他全做对了。

2 老师很高兴，同时也十分惊讶。

3 他把蒂姆叫到桌前说："蒂姆，你这次的作业全都做对了，怎么回事？你爸爸帮你做了吗？"

4 "没有，先生，我爸爸昨天很忙，我不得不全由自己做。"蒂姆说到。

## 爆笑故事

1 One day, Tim's mathematics teacher looked at his homework and saw that he had got all his sums right.

2 The teacher was very pleased and rather surprised.

3 He called Tim to his desk and said to him, "You got all your homework right this time, Tim. What happened? Did your father help you?"

4 "No, sir, he was too busy last night, so I had to do it all myself." said Tim.

## 生词宝库

mathematics [mæθˈmætɪks] *n.* 数学（等于 maths）

sum [sʌm] *n.* 算术题

pleased [pliːzd] *adj.* 高兴的

surprised [səˈpraɪzd] *adj.* 感到惊讶的

desk [desk] *n.* 办公桌

# I Hung Him Up to Dry
# 我把他吊起来好让他晾干

1 Jim and Mary were both patients in a Mental Hospital. One day while they were walking by the hospital swimming pool, Jim suddenly jumped into the deep end. He sank to the bottom. Mary promptly jumped in to save him. She swam to the bottom and pulled Jim out.

2 When the medical director became aware of Mary's heroic act he immediately reviewed her file and called her into his office.

3 "Mary, I have good news and bad news. The good news is you're being discharged because since you were able to jump in and save the life of another patient, I think you've regained your senses. The bad news is Jim, the patient you saved, hung himself with his bathrobe belt in the bathroom, he's dead."

4 Mary replied, "He didn't hang himself, I hung him up to dry."

1 吉姆和玛丽都是精神病院里的病人。一天，他们沿着医院的游泳池散步，吉姆突然跳入泳池的深水区，他沉到了底部。玛丽立刻跳下去救他，她潜到水底，把吉姆拉了上来。

2 当院长听闻了玛丽的英勇行为后，他立刻翻看了她的病历档案，把她叫进了自己的办公室。

3 "玛丽，我有一个好消息和一个坏消息要告诉你。好消息是你能跳入水中救其他病人，这说明你的意识已经恢复了，你可以出院了。坏消息就是，吉姆，你救的那个病人，他还是用自己的浴袍带子在浴室上吊自杀了。"

4 玛丽说："他没有自杀，是我把他吊起来好让他晾干的。"

## 生词宝库

patient [ˈpeɪʃnt] *n.* 病人

swimming pool 游泳池

bottom [ˈbɒtəm] *n.* 底部

medical [ˈmedɪkl] *adj.* 医疗的

heroic [hɪˈrəʊɪk] *adj.* 英雄的；英勇的

review [rɪˈvjuː] *v.* 回顾；检查

discharge [dɪsˈtʃɑːdʒ] *v.* 允许离开（医院、军队、监狱等）

regain [rɪˈgeɪn] *v.* 恢复

bathrobe [ˈbɑːθrəʊb] *n.* 浴衣

belt [belt] *n.* 带；腰带

# Two Steaks
# 两份牛排

1 One day, Bill and Tom went to a restaurant for dinner. As soon as the waiter took out two steaks, Bill quickly picked out the bigger steak for himself.

2 Tom wasn't happy about that: "When are you going to learn to be polite?"

3 Bill: "If you had the chance to pick first, which one would you pick?"

4 Tom: "The smaller piece, of course."

5 Bill: "What are you whining about then? The smaller piece is what you want, right?"

## 点睛译文

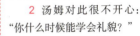

1 一天，比尔和汤姆去餐馆吃饭。当服务员端上两份牛排时，比尔迅速地为自己拿了比较大的那块。

2 汤姆对此很不开心："你什么时候能学会礼貌？"

3 比尔说："如果让你先拿，你会拿哪个？"

4 汤姆说："当然是小的那个。"

5 比尔："那你还抱怨什么？小的那个不就正是你想要的，不是吗？"

waiter [ˈweɪtə] *n.*（男）服务员

steak [steɪk] *n.* 牛排

polite [pəˈlaɪt] *adj.* 有礼貌的

# Keep the Job
# 保住工作

## 点睛译文

1 这个病人显得很坚决。

2 “医生，我需要做肝脏移植、肾脏移植、心脏移植、角膜移植、脾脏移植、胰腺移植和……”

3 “你为什么认为你需要做这么多移植手术？”

4 病人回答：“哦，是这样，我的老板说如果我这个人不重新组装的话，就别想保住我的工作！”

## 爆笑故事

1 The patient is adamant.

2 “Doc, I need a liver transplant, a kidney transplant, a heart transplant, a cornea transplant, a spleen transplant, a pancreas trans…”

3 “What makes you think you need all these?”

4 “Well,” replied the patient, “My boss said if I wanted to keep my job I needed to get reorganized.”

## 生词宝库

adamant [ˈædəmənt] *adj.* 固执的
liver [ˈlɪvə] *n.* 肝脏
transplant [ˈtrænsplɑːnt] *n.* 移植
kidney [ˈkɪdnɪ] *n.* 肾
cornea [ˈkɔːnɪə] *n.* 角膜
spleen [spliːn] *n.* 脾脏
pancreas [ˈpæŋkrɪəs] *n.* 胰腺

# Don't Ever Do That Again

# 别再这么干了

1 A taxi passenger tapped the driver on the shoulder to ask him a question. The driver screamed, lost control of the car, nearly hit a bus, went up on the footpath, and stopped centimeters from a shop window.

2 The driver said, "Look mate, don't ever do that again. You scared the daylights out of me!"

3 The passenger apologized and said, "I didn't realize that a little tap would scare you so much."

4 The driver replied, "Sorry, it's not really your fault. Today is my first day as a cab driver. I've been driving a funeral van for the last 25 years."

1 乘客轻拍了一下出租车司机的肩膀，想问个问题。司机大叫起来，车也失去了控制，几乎撞上一辆公车，还上了便道，在还差几厘米就撞上商店橱窗时终于停了下来。

2 司机说："伙计，别再这么干了。你把我吓破胆了！"

3 乘客抱歉地说："我没想到拍你一下就吓成这样。"

4 司机说："对不起，也不全是你的错。今天是我第一天开出租。以前 25 年里我一直开殡葬车。"

## 生词宝库

tap [tæp] *v.* 轻拍

shoulder [ˈʃəʊldə] *n.* 肩膀

hit [hɪt] *v.* 撞击

footpath [ˈfʊtpɑːθ] *n.* 小径

centimeter [ˈsentɪmiːtə] *n.* 厘米

fault [fɔːlt] *n.* 错误

funeral [ˈfjuːnərəl] *adj.* 丧葬的

van [væn] *n.* 厢式货车

# Did the Same Thing
# 做了同样的事

## 点睛译文

1 我赶着开车将11岁的女儿送到学校去，在红灯处右拐了，而那是不允许的（译注：在一些国家如英国，其交通规则是车辆左行的，与我国相反）。

2 “啊噢。”意识到犯了错误，我说，“我刚才拐弯是违章的。”

3 “我想那没关系的，妈妈。”女儿回答说，“我们后面的警车也同样拐了弯。”

## 爆笑故事

1 Hurrying my 11-year old daughter to school, I made a right turn at a red light when it was prohibited.

2 “Uh-oh.” I said, realizing my mistake, “I just make an illegal turn.”

3 “I guess it’s all right, mom.” my daughter replied, “The police car behind us did the same thing.”

## 生词宝库

turn [tɜːn] *n.* 转弯

prohibite [prəˈhɪbɪt] *v.* 禁止

illegal [ɪˈliːgl] *adj.* 非法的

behind [bɪˈhaɪnd] *prep.* 在……之后

# They're All Widows Now

# 她们都成寡妇了

## 爆笑故事

1 Uncle Frank, at 79, was a healthy and wealthy man, a lifelong bachelor. He courted a lot, he said, but "never boiled over — just simmered."

2 On a whim, he decided to take a trip around the country to look up nearly a dozen old girlfriends.

3 Upon his return he exclaimed, "Whew! Thank goodness I never married any of those women — They're all widows now!"

## 点睛译文

1 弗兰克叔叔78岁了，富有而健康。他终生都是个单身汉。他曾追求过很多女孩，但"从不过热——见好就收"。

2 一天他突发奇想，决定四处走走，去看看他那些接近一打的旧时女友。

3 他回来即叹道："嘘！谢天谢地，幸亏我没娶那些女人中的任何一个。如今她们都成寡妇了！"

## 生词宝库

healthy [ˈhelθɪ] *adj.* 健康的

wealthy [ˈwelθɪ] *adj.* 富有的

lifelong [ˈlaɪflɒŋ] *adj.* 终身的

bachelor [ˈbætʃələ] *n.* 单身汉

simmer [ˈsɪmə] *v.* 使保持在即将沸腾状态

court [kɔːt] *v.* 招致；追求

whim [wɪm] *n.* 一时的兴致

widow [ˈwɪdəʊ] *n.* 寡妇

# Soldier and Officer

# 士兵与军官

1 第一次世界大战期间，一场大战役正在进行。枪炮轰鸣，炮弹和子弹到处乱飞。这样过了一个小时后，一个士兵认定战斗对他来说变得太危险了，所以他离开前线开始逃离战场。步行了一个小时之后，他看见一个军官向他走过来。

2 那军官叫住他说："你要到哪儿去？"

3 "长官，我正尽可能远地躲开我们身后正在进行的战役。"士兵回答说。

4 "你知道我是谁吗？"军官生气地对他说，"我是你的指挥官。"

5 那士兵听到此话感到非常惊讶，说："天哪，想不到我已经往回跑了这么远了！"

1 A big battle was going on during the First World War. Guns were firing, and shells and bullets were flying about everywhere. After an hour of this, one of the soldiers decided that the fighting was getting too dangerous for him, so he left the front line and began to go away from the battle. After he had walked for an hour, he saw an officer coming towards him.

2 The officer stopped him and said, "Where are you going?"

3 "I'm trying to get as far away as possible from the battle that's going on behind us, sir." the soldier answered.

4 "Do you know who I am?" the officer said to him angrily,"I'm your commanding officer."

5 The soldier was very surprised when he heard this and said, "My God, I didn't know that I was so far back already!"

battle [ˈbætl] *n.* 战斗
shell [ʃel] *n.* 炮壳
bullet [ˈbʊlɪt] *n.* 子弹
dangerous [ˈdeɪndʒərəs] *adj.* 危险的
officer [ˈɒfɪsə] *n.* 军官
angrily [ˈæŋgrəlɪ] *adv.* 气愤地

# A Painter

# 油漆匠

## 点睛译文

1 一个富有的主妇为她收藏了一件非常有价值的古董花瓶感到很是骄傲，于是她决定把卧室粉刷成与花瓶同样的颜色。许多油漆匠都试图尽力匹配花瓶的颜色，但是没有任何人能做得让那古怪的女人满意。

2 一个油漆匠很自信他能做到，最终他成功了。那个主妇很满意，于是这个油漆匠也变得很出名。

3 多年以后，油漆匠要退休了，他把自己的生意交给儿子去经营。

4 “爸爸，”儿子问，“我还有些事情想知道，你怎么能把墙粉刷得和花瓶的颜色那么相配呢？”

5 “儿子，”爸爸回答道，“我只不过是把花瓶刷了。”

## 爆笑故事

1 A wealthy matron is so proud of a valuable antique vase that she decides to have her bedroom painted the same color as the vase. Several painters try to match the shade, but none comes close enough to satisfy the eccentric woman.

2 Eventually, a painter approaches who is confident he can mix the proper color. The woman is pleased with the result, and the painter becomes famous.

3 Years later, he retires and turns the business over to his son.

4 “Dad,” says the son, “there’s something I’ve got to know. How did you get those walls to match the vase so perfectly?”

5 “Son,” the father replies, “I painted the vase.”

## 生词宝库

matron [ˈmeɪtrən] *n.* 主妇

valuable [ˈvæljʊəbl] *adj.* 贵重的

antique [ænˈtiːk] *n.* 古董

vase [vɑːz] *n.* 花瓶

shade [ʃeɪd] *n.*（色泽的）明暗，深浅；明暗度

satisfy [ˈsætɪsfaɪ] *v.* 使满意

eccentric [ɪkˈsentrɪk] *adj.* 古怪的

proper [ˈprɒpə] *adj.* 适当的

retire [rɪˈtaɪə] *v.* 退休

# Napoleon Was Ill

# 拿破仑病了

## 点睛译文

1 杰克到一所大学去学历史。第一学期结束时，历史课教授没让他及格，学校让他退学。然而，杰克的父亲决定去见教授，强烈要求让杰克继续来年的学业。

2 “他是个好孩子。”杰克的父亲说，“您要是让他这次及格，我相信他明年会有很大进步，学期结束时，他一定会考好的。”

3 “不，不，那不可能。”教授马上回答，“你知道吗？上个月我问他拿破仑什么时候死的，他都不知道。”

4 “先生，请再给他一次机会吧。”杰克的父亲说，“你不知道，恐怕是因为我们家没有订报纸，我们家的人连拿破仑病了都不知道。”

## 爆笑故事

1 Jack had gone to the university to study history, but at the end of his first year, his history professor failed him in his examinations, and he was told that he would have to leave the university. However, his father decided that he would go to see the professor to urge him to let Jack continue his studies the following year.

2 “He’s a good boy.” said Jack’s father, “and if you let him pass this time, I’m sure he’ll improve a lot next year and pass the examinations at the end of it really well.”

3 “No, no, that’s quite impossible.” replied the professor immediately. “Do you know, last month I asked him when Napoleon had died, he didn’t know!”

4 “Please, sir, give him another chance.” said Jack’s father, “You see, I’m afraid we don’t take any newspaper in our house, so none of us even know that Napoleon was ill.”

history [ˈhɪstərɪ] *n.* 历史

university [ˌjuːnɪˈvɜːsətɪ] *n.* 大学

decide [dɪˈsaɪd] *v.* 决定

urge [ɜːdʒ] *v.* 催促

improve [ɪmˈpruːv] *v.* 改善

# I Am the Groom
# 我是新郎

## 点睛译文

1 大街上的一个超速驾驶者被警察拦住了。

2 “但是警官，”这个人说道，“我可以解释的。”

3 “保持安静。”警察打断了他，“我将把你送往监狱，直到长官回来。”

4 “但是，警察，我……”

5 “我说过了保持安静，你要到监狱了。”

6 几小时后，警察向监狱里看了看说道：“算你运气好，因为我们的长官正在他女儿的婚礼上呢，他会带着愉快的心情回来的。”

7 “你确定？”在牢房里的这个人说道，“我是新郎。”

## 爆笑故事

1 A police stopped a motorist who was speeding on the street.

2 “But officer,” the man said, “I can explain.”

3 “Just be quiet.” snapped the officer, “I'm going to put you in jail until the chief gets back.”

4 “But, officer, I …”

5 “I said to keep quiet! You are going to jail!”

6 A few hours later, the officer looked in on his prisoner and said, “You are lucky because the chief is at his daughter's wedding. He'll be in a good mood when he gets back.”

7 “Are you sure?” answered the man in the cell. “I'm the groom.”

## 生词宝库

motorist [ˈməutərɪst] *n.* 驾车的人

speed [spiːd] *v.* 超速行驶

snap [snæp] *v.* 厉声说

chief [tʃiːf] *n.* 首领；长官

prisoner [ˈprɪznə] *n.* 囚犯

lucky [ˈlʌkɪ] *adj.* 幸运的

wedding [ˈwedɪŋ] *n.* 婚礼

mood [muːd] *n.* 情绪

cell [sel] *n.* 单人牢房

groom [gruːm] *n.* 新郎

# A Lawyer's Dog

# 律师的狗

## 爆笑故事

1 A lawyer's dog, running about unleashed, beelines for a butcher shop and steals a roast. Butcher goes to lawyer's office and asks, "If a dog running unleashed steals a piece of meat from my store, do I have a right to demand payment for the meat from the dog's owner?"

2 The lawyer answers, "Absolutely."

3 "Then you owe me $8.50. Your dog was loose and stole a roast from me today."

4 The lawyer, without a word, writes the butcher a check for $8.50.

5 Several days later, the butcher opens the mail and finds an envelope from the lawyer: $250 due for a consultation.

## 点睛译文

1 律师的狗，没有拴着到处闲逛。它来到一家肉店，偷走了一块烤肉。店主来到律师的办公室，问道："如果一条没栓的狗从我的商店里偷了块肉，我有权利从狗的主人那里要回损失吗？"

2 律师答道："完全可以。"

3 "那你欠我8.5美元，你的狗没栓，而且今天从我的店里偷了块肉。"

4 律师什么都没说，马上给他写了一张支票。

5 几天后，店主打开邮箱，发现一封来自律师的信，信上写道：咨询费250美元。

## 生词宝库

unleash [ʌnˈliːʃ] *v.* 解开……的皮带

butcher [ˈbʊtʃə] *n.* 屠夫

roast [rəʊst] *n.* 烤肉

loose [luːs] *adj.* 不加限制的，松的

consultation [ˌkɒnslˈteɪʃn] *n.* 咨询

# Boss's Idea
# 老板的主意

## 点睛译文

1 由于我的打印机不能打印出清晰的字来，我就打电话给维修部。电话是一个非常和蔼的男人接的，他说我的打印机也许只是需要清理一下。

2 他还说，如果让维修部清理的话。要交50英镑的清理费，让我最好看看使用手册自己试着清理。

3 当时我真的被他的话感动了，就问他："你们老板知道你这样拒绝生意吗？"

4 "事实上，这就是我们老板的主意。"雇员答道，"因为如果我们让用户先自行修理打印机，就能挣更多的钱。"

1 When my printer's type began to go faint, I called a repair shop where a friendly man told me that the printer probably needed only to be cleaned.

2 Because the shop charged 50 pounds for such cleanings, he told me, it would be better for me to read the printer's directions and try the job myself.

3 Pleasantly surprised by his words, I asked, "Does your boss know that you discourage business?"

4 "Actually it's my boss's idea." the employee replied, "We usually make more money on repairs if we let people try to repair things themselves first."

## 生词宝库

printer [ˈprɪntə] *n.* 打印机
faint [feɪnt] *adj.* 模糊的
repair [rɪˈpeə] *n.* 维修
charge [tʃɑːdʒ] *v.* 要价
directions [dɪˈrekʃənz] *n.* 用法说明书
discourage [dɪsˈkʌrɪdʒ] *v.* 劝阻
employee [emplɒɪˈiː] *n.* 雇员

# They Are Directly from America
# 它们是从美国直接带来的

## 爆笑故事

1 Not long after an old Chinese woman came back to China from her visit to her daughter in the States, she went to a city bank to deposit the US dollars her daughter gave her. At the bank counter, the clerk checked each note carefully to see if the money was real.

2 It made the old lady out of patience. At last she could not hold any more, uttering, "Trust me, sir, and trust the money. They are real US dollars. They are directly from America."

## 点睛译文

1 一位中国老妇人在美国看望女儿回来不久，到一家市银行存女儿给她的美元。在银行柜台，银行职员认真检查了每一张钞票，看是否有假。

2 这种做法让老妇人很不耐烦，最后实在忍耐不住说："相信我，先生，也请你相信这些钞票。这都是真正的美元，它们是从美国直接带来的。"

## 生词宝库

deposit [dɪˈpɒzɪt] *v.* 存储

counter [ˈkaʊntə] *n.* 柜台

note [nəʊt] *n.* 纸币

directly [dəˈrektlɪ] *adv.* 直接地

# The Doctor Lives Downstairs
# 医生住在楼下

## 点睛译文

1 “医生！”她冲进屋后大声说道，“我想让你坦率地说我到底得了什么病。”

2 他从头到脚打量打量她，然后大声说：“太太，我有三件事要对你说。第一，您的体重需要减少大约 50 磅；第二，如果您只用十分之一的胭脂和口红，您会变得更美。第三，我是一位画家——医生住在楼下。”

## 爆笑故事

1 “Doctor!” she said loudly, bouncing into the room, “I want you to say frankly what’s wrong with me.”

2 He surveyed her from head to foot. “Madam,” he said at length, “I’ve just three things to tell you. First, your weight wants reducing by nearly fifty pounds. Second, your beauty could be improved if you used about one tenth as much rouge and lipstick. And third, I’m an artist — the doctor lives downstairs.”

## 生词宝库

bounce [baʊns] *v.* 冲进
frankly [ˈfræŋklɪ] *adv.* 坦率地
survey [ˈsɜːveɪ] *v.* 审视
weight [weɪt] *n.* 体重
reducing [rɪˈduːsɪŋ] *n.* 减低
rouge [ruːʒ] *n.* 胭脂
lipstick [ˈlɪpstɪk] *n.* 口红

# Mixed Doubles

# 混合双打

1 Teacher of Physical Education: Have you ever seen mixed doubles, boys?

2 Nick: Yes, sir. Quite of ten. I saw it even last night.

3 Teacher: Please tell us some thing about it.

4 Nick: Oh, sorry, sir. My father always says, "Domestic shame should not be published."

点睛译文

1 体育老师：孩子们，你们见过男女混合双打吗？

2 尼克：见过，老师，经常见。就在昨天夜里我还见过呢！

3 老师：那你给大家讲讲当时的情形吧。

4 尼克：啊，对不起，老师。我爸爸常说："家丑不可外扬。"

physical [ˈfɪzɪkəl] *adj.* 身体的

mixed double 混双

domestic [dəˈmestɪk] *adj.* 家里的

shame [ʃeɪm] *n.* 羞耻

publish [ˈpʌblɪʃ] *v.* 公布

# $50

# 50美元

点睛译文

1 有个小男孩非常需要50美元，他为此祷告了数周，但是什么也没发生。后来，他决定写封信向上帝索要这50美元。

2 邮局接到这封信，想了想觉得还是应该交给总统比较好。总统被逗笑了，于是指示秘书寄给小男孩5美元，因为他觉得5美元对于一个小孩来讲已经是不少了。

3 小男孩收到钱了很高兴，给上帝回了一封感谢信，信里写道：

4 “尊敬的上帝：非常感谢你把钱寄给我。然而，我发现这些钱是通过白宫寄出的，因此，和往常一样，那帮家伙收了我45美元的税。”

1 A little boy needed $50 very badly and prayed for weeks, but nothing happened. Then he decided to write God a letter requesting the $50.

2 When the post office received the letter to God, USA, they decided to send it to the president. The president was so amused that he instructed his secretary to send the boy a $5 bill. The president thought this would appear to be a lot of money to a little boy.

3 The little boy was delighted with the $5 bill and sat down to write a thank-you note to God, which read:

4 “Dear God: Thank you very much for sending the money. However, I noticed that for some reason you sent it through Washington, D.C., and, as usual, those turkeys kept $45 in taxes.”

badly [ˈbædlɪ] *adv.* <口>非常，很，极

request [rɪˈkwest] *v.* 索要

post office 邮局

amused [əˈmjuːzd] *adj.* 被逗乐的

president [ˈprezɪdənt] *n.* 总统

delighted [dɪˈlaɪtɪd] *adj.* 高兴的

turkey [ˈtɜːkɪ] *n.* 不起作用的家伙

tax [tæks] *n.* 税金

# A Ground Rule
# 一条课堂纪律

## 爆笑故事

1 One of my favorite teachers at Southeast Missouri State University in Cape Girardeau is known for his droll sense of humor.

2 Explaining his ground rules to one freshman class, he said, "Now I know my lectures can often be dry and boring, so I don't mind if you look at your watches during class. I do, however, object to your pounding them on the desk to make sure they're running!"

## 点睛译文

1 在开普吉拉多市的东南密苏里州立大学上学的时候，我喜欢的几个老师之中有一个以他的幽默感而出名。

2 给新生上头一节课时，他给学生解释在他课上的纪律，他说："我知道我的课经常会很枯燥乏味，所以我并不介意你们在课上看表。然而，我坚决不允许你们把表重重地摔在课桌上，以此来检查你们的表是不是还在走。"

## 生词宝库

favorite [ˈfeɪvərɪt] *adj.* 喜爱的

droll [drəʊl] *adj.* 好笑的

humor [ˈhjuːmə] *n.* 幽默

freshman [ˈfreʃmən] *n.* 大学一年级学生

lecture [ˈlektʃə] *n.* 讲课

dry [draɪ] *adj.* 枯燥无味的

boring [ˈbɔːrɪŋ] *adj.* 令人厌烦的

pound [paʊnd] *v.* 敲打；猛击

# Captain's Recording

# 机长的录音

1 This is your captain speaking.

2 On behalf of my crew, I'd like to welcome you aboard British Airways flight 602 from New York to London. We are currently flying at a height of 35,000 feet midway across the Atlantic. If you look out of the windows on the starboard side of the aircraft, you will observe that both the starboard engines are on fire. If you look out of the windows on the port side, you will observe that the port wing has fallen off. If you look down towards the Atlantic Ocean, you will see a little yellow life raft with three people in it to waving at you. That's me, the copilot, and one of the air stewardesses.

3 This is a recording.

1 我是机长。

2 请允许我代表全体工作人员，欢迎你们乘坐英国航空公司从纽约飞往伦敦的 602 号航班。我们此时在大西洋上空 35000 英尺的高度。如果你从飞机的右边向窗外看去，你将会发现右侧的两个引擎都已经起火。如果你从左边往外看，你就会看到那边的机翼已经脱落了。如果你俯视下面的大西洋，那么你会看到一艘黄色的救生筏，上面有 3 个人正在朝你挥手。那是我、副驾驶员还有我们的一名女乘务员。

3 这是一段录音。

生词宝库

captain [ˈkæptɪn] *n.* 机长

on behalf of 代表

crew [kruː] *n.* 全体乘务员

starboard [ˈstɑːbəd] *n.*【空】右舷

observe [əbˈzɜːv] *v.* 注意到

port [pɔːt] *n.* 左舷

raft [rɑːft] *n.* 筏

copilot [ˈkəʊˌpaɪlət] *n.* 副驾驶员

# What's Time to a Pig
# 时间对猪有什么意义

## 点睛译文

1 一天，有一个城市里的游客来到一个小乡村，在乡间路上开着车，想看看农庄是什么样子，也想看看农夫怎样过日子。这位城里人看见一位农夫在宅后的草地上，手中抱着一头猪，并把它举得高高的，好让它能够吃到树上的苹果。

2 城里人对农夫说："我看你的猪挺喜欢吃苹果的，但是，这不是很浪费时间吗？"

3 那位农夫回答说："时间对猪有什么意义？"

## 爆笑故事

1 One day a visitor from the city came to a small rural area to drive around the country roads, see how the farms looked, and perhaps to see how farmers earned their living. The city man saw a farmer in his yard, holding a pig up in his hands, and lifting it so that the pig could eat apples from an apple tree.

2 The city man said to the farmer: "I see that your pig likes apples, but isn't that quite a waste of time?"

3 The farmer replied: "What's time to a pig?"

## 生词宝库

rural [ˈrʊərəl] *adj.* 农村的

country [ˈkʌntrɪ] *adj.* 乡村的

perhaps [pəˈhæps] *adv.* 也许

earn [ɜːn] *v.* 挣得

yard [jɑːd] *n.* 院子

# A Brain Transplant
# 脑移植

## 爆笑故事

1 The Brain Surgeon was about to perform a brain transplant.

2 "You have your choice of two brains." he told the patient, "For $1000 you can have the brain of a psychologist, or for $10,000 you can have the brain of a politician."

3 The patient was amazed at the huge difference in price. "Is the brain of a politician that much better?" he asked.

4 The Brain Surgeon replied: "No, it's not better, just unused."

## 点睛译文

1 一个外科医生正要做一个脑移植手术。

2 "你可以从两个脑子中选一个。"医生告诉病人，"一个心理学家的大脑1000美元，一个政治家的大脑10000美元。"

3 病人很惊讶二者之间有这样大的差别，"政治家的大脑好一些吗？"他问。

4 医生说："不是好一些，只是没有用过。"

## 生词宝库

surgeon [ˈsɜːdʒən] *n.* 外科医生

perform [pəˈfɔːm] *v.* 进行

choice [tʃɔɪs] *n.* 选择

psychologist [saɪˈkɒlədʒɪst] *n.* 心理学家

politician [pɒlɪˈtɪʃən] *n.* 政治家

# Isn't It Wonderful
# 这难道不好吗

## 点睛译文

1 “你为什么事这么高兴？”一个女士问一个98岁的老人。

2 “我打碎了一个镜子。”他回答。

3 “但那预示着7年的坏运气。”

4 “我知道。”他高兴地说，“这难道不好吗？”

## 爆笑故事

1 “What are you so happy about?” a woman asked the 98-year-old man.

2 “I broke a mirror.” he replied.

3 “But that means seven years of bad luck.”

4 “I know.” he said, beaming, “Isn't it wonderful?”

## 生词宝库

broke [brəʊk] *v.* 打碎（动词break的过去式）

mirror [ˈmɪrə] *n.* 镜子

luck [lʌk] *n.* 运气

beaming [ˈbiːmɪŋ] *adj.* 笑盈盈的

wonderful [ˈwʌndəfʊl] *adj.* 极好的

# If I Am a Manager
# 如果我是经理

## 爆笑故事

1 One day in class, the teacher assigned his students to write a composition — If I Am a Manager.

2 All the students began to write except a boy. The teacher went to him and asked the reason.

3 "I am waiting for my secretary." was the boy's answer.

## 点睛译文

1 一天的课上，老师要同学们以《如果我是经理》为题写一篇作文。

2 所有的学生都在动笔写了，只有一个男生例外。老师走过去问他为什么不写。

3 "我在等我的秘书。"那孩子答道。

## 生词宝库

assign [ə'saɪn] *v.* 指定

composition [ˌkɒmpə'zɪʃn] *n.* 作文

except [ɪk'sept] prep. 除了……之外

reason ['ri:zən] *n.* 理由

secretary ['sekrɪtərɪ] *n.* 秘书

# A Man of Actions
# 一个言出必行的人

1 一群学生聚在牛津的校园里，一个年轻人情绪激动地叫道："毋庸置疑，如果那个院长家伙不收回他今早对我说的话，我今晚就离开牛津。"

2 下面一片喧哗。"真是个言出必行的人。"一个人艳羡地说。

3 另一个说："我们要支持他、向他学习。"

4 突然，一个女孩问道："院长对你说什么了，霍波？"

5 他弯下腰小声说："哦，呃……呃……，罗斯小姐，呃……他说要我今晚从牛津滚出去。"

1 A crowd of student was gathered on the campus of Oxford University. "You can have no doubt," shouted a young man excitedly, "that if the Dean does not take back what he said to me this morning, I'll leave Oxford this very evening!"

2 A buzzing noise followed. "What a man of actions!" one said in admiration.

3 "How should we support him and learn from him!" said another.

4 Suddenly, a girl asked, "What did the Dean say to you, Hob?"

5 He bent and whispered to her, "Well, er… er… Miss Rose, er… he told me to get clean away from Oxford this very evening!"

**生词宝库**

crowd [kraʊd] *n.* 人群
gather [ˈgæðə] *v.* 聚集
Oxford [ˈɒksfəd] *n.* 牛津大学
doubt [daʊt] *n.* 怀疑
action [ˈækʃən] *n.* 行动
admiration [ædməˈreɪʃən] *n.* 钦佩；赞赏
bend [bend] *v.* 弯腰

# The Fourth Element

# 第四元素

1 Teacher: What are the four element of nature?

2 Student: Fire, air, earth, and... and ...

3 Teacher: And what? Just think it over; what do you wash your hands with?

4 Student: Soap!

1 老师：自然界的四大元素是什么？

2 学生：火、气、土和……和……

3 老师：和什么？想一想，你用什么洗手的？

4 学生：肥皂。

生词宝库

element [ˈelɪmənt] *n.* 元素

nature [ˈneɪtʃə] *n.* 自然界

wash [wɒʃ] *v.* 洗

soap [səʊp] *n.* 肥皂

# Make Your Future
# 计划你的将来

1 “你以前是怎么计划你的将来的？”

2 “我以前计划要变成一个富人的合伙人，他有钱，我有经验。”

3 “结果呢？”

4 “现在他有经验了，我有钱。”

1 “How did you make your future?”

2 “I became the partner of a rich man. He had the money and I had the experience.”

3 “How did that help?”

4 “Now he has the experience and I the money.”

future [ˈfjuːtʃə] *n.* 将来

partner [ˈpɑːtnə] *n.* 合伙人

money [ˈmʌnɪ] *n.* 钱

experience [ɪkˈspɪərɪəns] *n.* 经验

# Boxing and Running

# 拳击和赛跑

## 爆笑故事

1 Dan is teaching his son how to box. As he does so, he told his friend, “This is a tough world, so I’m teaching my boy to fight.”

2 Friend: “But suppose he comes up against someone much bigger than he is, who’s also been taught how to box.”

3 Dan: “I’m teaching him how to run, too.”

## 点睛译文

1 丹在教他的儿子怎样拳击。他告诉他的朋友：“这是一个残酷的世界，所以我要教我的儿子怎么去拼搏。”

2 朋友：“如果他碰上的对手是一个比他高大、健壮而且也会拳击的人怎么办？”

3 丹：“我也正在教他怎么样赛跑呢。”

## 生词宝库

box [bɒks] *v.* 拳击

tough [tʌf] *adj.* 艰难的

fight [faɪt] *v.* 奋斗；搏斗

suppose [səˈpəʊz] *v.* 假定

someone [ˈsʌmwʌn] *pron.* 某人

# The Looney Bin

# 疯人院

## 点睛译文

1 一天晚上，在疯人院里，一个病人喊道："我是拿破仑！"另一个说："你怎么知道？"

2 第一个人说："上帝对我说的！"

3 一会儿，一个声音从另一个房间传来："我没说！"

## 爆笑故事

1 Late one night at the insane asylum one inmate shouted, "I am Napoleon!"Another one said, "How do you know?"

2 The first inmate said, "God told me!"

3 Just then, a voice from another room shouted, "I did not!"

## 生词宝库

insane [ɪn'seɪn] *n.* 精神失常的人

asylum [ə'saɪləm] *n.* 精神病院

inmate ['ɪnmeɪt] *n.* 同病房者

shout [ʃaʊt] *v.* 呼喊

# All I Do Is Pay

# 我要做的一切就是付钱

1 "My family is just like a nation," Mr. Brown told his colleague. "My wife is the minister of finance, my mother-in-law is the minister of war, and my daughter is foreign secretary."

2 "Sounds interesting." his colleague replied, "And what is your position?"

3 "I'm the people. All I do is pay."

## 点睛译文

1 布朗先生告诉同事说："我的家简直就像一个国家一样。我妻子是财政部长，我岳母是作战部长，我女儿是外交秘书。"

2 "听上去挺有意思的，"他的同事说，"那你的职务是什么呢？"

3 "我就是老百姓。我要做的一切就是付钱。"

## 生词宝库

nation [ˈneɪʃn] *n.* 国家

colleague [ˈkɒliːg] *n.* 同事

minister [ˈmɪnɪstə] *n.* 部长

finance [faɪˈnæns] *n.* 财政

position [pəˈzɪʃn] *n.* 职位

# For the Dog

# 喂狗

1 一家人在饭馆里吃过晚饭，父亲把服务生叫了过来。

2 “先生，什么事？”服务生问。

3 “我儿子的盘子里剩下许多肉。”父亲说，“能给我们一个袋子吗？我把剩下的东西带回去喂狗。”

4 “啊呀，爸爸！”儿子激动地叫喊着，“咱家养狗了吗？”

1 The family seated in a restaurant had finished their dinner when Father called over the waiter.

2 “May I help you, sir?” the waiter asked.

3 “My son has left quite a lot of meat on his plate.” explained Father, “Could you give me a bag so that I can take it home for the dog?”

4 “Gosh, Dad!” exclaimed the excited boy. “Have we got a dog then?”

生词宝库

seat [siːt] *v.* 坐

meat [miːt] *n.* 肉

plate [pleɪt] *n.* 碟

gosh [gɒʃ] int. 唉；糟了

# You Are Too Late
# 你太晚了

1 On the bus a man discovered a pickpocket's hand thrust into his pocket.

2 "Sorry." he said to the pickpocket, "you are too late. My wife did it before you."

## 点睛译文

1 在公共汽车上一人发现一个小偷把手伸到了他的口袋里。

2 "对不起，"他对小偷说，"你太晚了，我妻子在你之前就做过同样的事情了。"

## 生词宝库

discover [dɪ'skʌvə] *v.* 发现

pickpocket ['pɪkpɒkɪt] *n.* 扒手

thrust [θrʌst] *v.* 插入

# Mental Deficiency
# 智力缺陷

1 "Would you mind telling me, Doctor," Bob asked, "how you detect a mental deficiency in somebody who appears completely normal?"

2 "Nothing is easier." he replied, "You ask him a simple question which everyone should answer with no trouble. If he hesitates, that puts you on the track."

3 "Well, What sort of question?"

4 "Well, you might ask him: Captain Cook made three trips around the world and died during one of them. Which one?"

5 Bob thought for a moment, and then said with a nervous laugh, "You wouldn't happen to have another example, would you? I must confess I don't know much about history."

点睛译文

1 "医生，你能不能告诉我，"鲍勃问，"对于一个看上去很正常的人，你是怎样判断出他有智力缺陷的呢？"

2 "再没有比这容易的了。"医生回答，"问他一个简单的问题，简单到所有人都知道答案，如果他回答得不干脆，那你就知道是怎么回事了。"

3 "那要问什么样的问题呢？"

4 "嗯，你可以这样问：库克船长环球旅行了3次，但是在其中一次的途中他去世了，是哪一次呢？"

5 鲍勃想了一会儿，紧张地回答道，"你就不能问另外一个问题吗？坦率地说，我对历史了解的不是很多。"

## 生词宝库

detect [dɪˈtekt] *v.* 察觉

mental [ˈmentəl] *adj.* 脑力的

deficiency [dɪˈfɪʃnsɪ] *n.* 缺陷

normal [ˈnɔːməl] *adj.* 正常的

simple [ˈsɪmpəl] *adj.* 简单的

hesitate [ˈhezɪteɪt] *v.* 犹豫

sort [sɔːt] *n.* 种类

nervous [ˈnɜːvəs] *adj.* 紧张的

example [ɪgˈzɑːmpəl] *n.* 例子

confess [kənˈfes] *v.* 承认

# Beware of Dog
# 小心有狗

## 点睛译文

1 一个陌生人走进一家乡间小商店，看到玻璃门上帖着的一个告示牌上写着，“危险！小心有狗！”进去后，他看到一条样子一点都不凶的老狗趴在收款机旁边的地板上睡觉。

2 “这就是大伙都得留神的那只狗啊？”陌生人问店主。

3 “是，就是他。”店主回答。

4 听到这个回答，陌生人觉得很好笑。“我觉得那条狗一点都不可怕。你帖那个告示做什么？”

5 “因为，”店主解释说，“在我帖告示之前，大伙老被他绊倒。”

## 爆笑故事

1 As a stranger entered a little country store, he noticed a sign warning, “Danger! Beware of dog!” posted on the glass door. Inside, he noticed a harmless old hound dog asleep on the floor beside the cash register.

2 “Is that the dog folks are supposed to beware of?” he asked the owner.

3 “Yep, that's him.” came the reply.

4 The stranger couldn't help but be amused. “That certainly doesn't look like a dangerous dog to me. Why in the world would you post that sign?”

5 “Because,” the owner explained, “Before I posted that sign, people kept tripping over him!”

## 生词宝库

stranger [ˈstreɪndʒə] *n.* 陌生人

store [stɔː] *n.* 商店

post [pəʊst] *v.* 张贴

harmless [ˈhaːmləs] *adj.* 无害的；无恶意的

hound [haʊnd] *n.* 猎狗

cash register [kæʃ ˈredʒistə] *n.* 收银机

folk [fəʊk] *n.* 人们

trip [trɪp] *v.* 绊倒

# I'll See to the Rest

# 其余的事由我负责

1 A guard was about to signal his train to start when he saw an attractive girl standing on the platform by an open door, talking to another pretty girl inside the carriage.

2 "Come on, miss!" he shouted. "Shut the door, please!"

3 "Oh, I just want to kiss my sister goodbye." she called back.

4 "You just shut that door, please." called the guard, "and I'll see to the rest."

1 一位车上的列车员刚要让火车启动，这时他看见一位很漂亮的姑娘站在站台上一节打开的车厢门旁边，跟车厢里另一位漂亮姑娘在说话。

2 "快点，小姐！" 他喊道："请把门关上。"

3 "噢，我还没有和妹妹吻别呢。" 她回答道。

4 "请把门关上好了，" 列车员说："其余的事由我负责。"

## 生词宝库

guard [gɑːd] *n.* <英> 列车长，列车员

attractive [əˈtræktɪv] *adj.* 有魅力的

platform [ˈplætfɔːm] *n.* 站台

carriage [ˈkærɪdʒ] *n.* 客车车厢

shut [ʃʌt] *v.* 关闭

# Friend for Dinner
# 请朋友吃饭

1 “亲爱的，”丈夫对妻子说：“我邀请了一位朋友回家吃晚饭。”

2 “什么？你疯了吗？我们的房子乱糟糟的，我很久没有买过东西回来了，所有的碗碟都是脏的，还有，我可不想做一餐累死人的晚饭。”

3 “这些我全都知道。”

4 “那你为什么还要邀请朋友回来吃晚饭？”

5 “因为那个可怜的笨蛋正考虑要结婚呢。”

1 “Honey,” said the husband to his wife, “I invited a friend home for supper.”

2 “What? Are you crazy? The house is a mess, I haven’t been shopping, all the dishes are dirty, and I don’t feel like cooking a fancy meal!”

3 “I know all that.”

4 “Then why did you invite a friend for supper?”

5 “Because the poor fool is thinking about getting married.”

## 生词宝库

supper [ˈsʌpə] *n.* 晚饭

mess [mes] *n.* 混乱

dish [dɪʃ] *n.* 盘；餐具

fancy [ˈfænsɪ] *adj.* 高难度的，花式的

# I Could Do It Slower

# 我可以干得慢一些

1 Patient: What do you charge for pulling a tooth?

2 Dentist: Fifty dollars.

3 Patient: Fifty dollars for a couple of minutes' work?

4 Dentist: Well, I could do it slower, if you like.

点睛译文

1 病人：拔一颗牙收费多少？

2 牙医：50 美元。

3 病人：只几分钟的活儿就要 50 美元？

4 牙医：好的，如果你喜欢的话，我可以干得慢一些。

pull [pʊl] *v.* 拔

a couple of 几个

slower [sləʊər] *adj.* 慢一点（形容词 slow 的比较级）

# No Cavities
# 我没有蛀牙

1 小男孩儿看完牙医，面带微笑地回到家：“嘿，妈妈，牙医说，我一颗蛀牙也没有。”

2 妈妈惊讶地瞪大眼睛：“不可能——你每回上床睡觉前都把巧克力盒子里的糖一下子吃完，而且从来不刷牙！”

3 这时，男孩儿张开了嘴巴——他的牙全被拔光了。

1 A smiling boy arrived home from a dental visit, “Hey mom, the dentist says I have no cavities.”

2 His mom stared at him wide-eyed and quite surprised, “It’s impossible — you never brush your teeth after cleaning the chocolate box before you go to bed!”

3 Then the boy opened his mouth — he had not a tooth left!

## 生词宝库

smiling [ˈsmaɪlɪŋ] *adj.* 喜气洋洋的

dental [ˈdentl] *adj.* 牙齿的；牙科的

cavity [ˈkævətɪ] *n.* 蛀洞

stare [steə] *v.* 盯着

# A New Employee

# 新员工

1 Several weeks after a young man had been hired, he was called into the personnel director's office.

2 "What is the meaning of this?" the director asked. "When you applied for the job, you told us you had five years' experience. Now we discover this is the first job you ever held."

3 "Well," the young man said, "in your advertisement you said you wanted somebody with imagination."

点睛译文

1 一个年轻人在被雇用几个星期后，被叫到人事经理的办公室。

2 "这是什么意思？"经理问，"当你申请这份工作时，你告诉我们有5年工作经验，现在我们发现这其实是你的第一份工作。"

3 "嗯，"年轻人回答，"你们的广告上说需要找一个有想象力的人嘛。"

生词宝库

personnel [ˌpɜːsəˈnel] *n.* 人事部门

director [dəˈrektə] *n.* 经理

advertisement [ədˈvɜːtɪzmənt] *n.* 广告

imagination [ɪˌmædʒɪˈneɪʃn] *n.* 想象

# To Be on the Safe Side

# 保证没走错

1 在一家电影院里，一名观众在演出期间站了起来，沿着他那排位子走到休息室去了。几分钟后，他回到那排位子并问坐在首位的那位男士道：

2 “对不起，请问我刚才出去的时候是踩着了你的脚吗？”

3 “是的，不过没什么关系，一点也不疼。”

4 “噢，不，我不是这个意思。我只是想确认一下这是不是我坐的那排位子。”

1 In a cinema during a performance one of the audiences gets up, makes his way along the row of seats and goes out into the foyer. A few minutes later he returns and asks the man sitting at the head of the row:

2 “Excuse me, was it your foot I stepped on when I was going out a moment ago?”

3 “Yes, but it doesn’t really matter. It didn’t hurt at all.”

4 “Oh, no, it isn’t that. I only want to make sure that this is my row.”

## 生词宝库

audience [ˈɔːdɪəns] *n.* 观众

foyer [ˈfɔɪeɪ] *n.* 休息室

row [rəʊ] *n.* 行，排

matter [ˈmætə] *v.* 有关系

make sure 弄明白

# Such a Long Dog
# 如此长的狗

1 Once there was a blind. One day when he was walking, he stepped the head of the dog who was sleeping. The dog barked for a while. The blind man went on for miles, this time he stepped the other dog's tail, so this dog barked. The blind man had thought that it was the first dog, so he said in surprise, "It's a wonder that the dog is so long."

点睛译文

1 从前有个瞎子。一天，他正在走路时，踩着了一只正在睡觉的狗的脑袋，狗汪汪汪地叫了一阵。这人又往前走，这回踩着的是另外一只狗的尾巴，狗又汪汪汪地叫起来。瞎子以为还是那条狗，惊诧地说："奇怪，这只狗可真够长的。"

生词宝库

blind [blaınd] *n.* 盲人

step [step] *v.* 踏

head [hed] *n.* 头

sleep [sliːp] *v.* 睡觉

# Good Wishes
# 美好心愿

1 One day a boy came to his teacher and said, "Teacher, pa wants to know if you like roast pig."

2 "I certainly do," said the teacher, "and you tell your father he is very kind to think of me."

3 Days passed, and nothing more was said about the roast pig.

4 Finally the teacher said to the boy, "I thought your father was going to send me over some roast pig."

5 "Yes," said the boy, "he did intend to, but the pig got well."

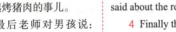

1 一天有个男孩去对他的老师说："老师，我爸想知道你是不是爱吃烤猪肉。"

2 "当然啰，"老师说，"去告诉你父亲，多谢他想着我。"

3 好几天过去了，男孩再没提起烤猪肉的事儿。

4 最后老师对男孩说："我以为你父亲要给我送点烤猪肉来呢。"

5 "是啊，"孩子说，"他是这么想的，可后来猪又没病了。"

生词宝库

pig [pɪg] *n.* 猪

think of 想到

pass [pɑːs] *v.* 过（时间）

intend [ɪn'tend] *v.* 想要

# Do You Know My Work
# 你知道我是干嘛的吗

点睛译文

1 One night a hotel caught fire, and people who were staying in it ran out in their night clothes.

2 Two men stood outside and looked at the fire.

3 "Before I came out," said one, "I ran into some of the rooms and found a lot of money. People don't think of money when they're afraid. When anyone leaves paper money in a fire, the fire burns it. So I took all the bills that I could find. No one will be poorer because I took them."

4 "You don't know my work," said the other.

5 "What is your work?"

6 "I'm a policeman."

7 "Oh!" cried the first man. He thought quickly and said, "And do you know my work?"

8 "No," said the policeman.

9 "I'm a writer. I'm always telling stories about things that never happened."

1 一天晚上，一家旅馆失火，住在这家旅馆里的人穿着睡衣就跑了出来。

2 两个人站在外面，看着大火。

3 "在我出来之前，"其中一个说，"我跑进一些房间，找到了一大笔钱。人在恐惧中是不会想到钱的。如果有人把纸币留在火里，火就会把它烧成灰烬，所以我把我所能找到的钞票都拿走了，没有人会因为我拿走它们而变得更穷。"

4 "你不知道我是干什么的。"另一个说。

5 "你是干什么的？"

6 "我是警察。"

7 "噢！"第一个人喊了一声，他灵机一动，说："那你知道我是干什么的？"

8 "不知道。"警察说。

9 "我是个作家，我总是爱编一些从未发生过的故事。"

## 生词宝库

hotel [həʊˈtel] *n.* 旅馆
outside [ˌaʊtˈsaɪd] *adv.* 在外面
room [ruːm] *n.* 房间
burn [bɜːn] *v.* 燃烧
work [wɜːk] *n.* 工作
writer [ˈraɪtə] *n.* 作家

# Rope or Ox
# 绳子还是公牛

1 The man in the prison asked a new comer why he was sent there. The new comer answered: "I am out of luck, I think. A few days ago I was walking in the street when I saw a piece of dirty rope. I thought nobody wanted it and so I picked it up and took it home."

2 "But it is not against the law to pick up a piece of rope and take home!"

3 "I told you I had bad luck, didn't I?" the man sighed, "The trouble is that I didn't notice there was an ox at the other end of that rope."

## 点睛译文

1 在监狱里，一个人问新来的犯人为什么被关进来。新来的犯人回答说："我想我真是倒霉。几天前我在街上走的时候，看到一根脏绳子，以为没人要了，便捡起来带了回家。"

2 "但是，捡一根绳子带回家并不犯法啊！"

3 "我告诉过你我倒霉了吧？"那个人叹了口气，"麻烦的就是我没有注意到绳子的那一头还有一头公牛。"

## 生词宝库

prison [ˈprɪzn] *n.* 监狱

comer [ˈkʌmə] *n.* 新来者

rope [rəʊp] *n.* 绳

ox [ɒks] *n.* 公牛

# Letter of Recommendation
# 推荐信

## 点睛译文

1 彼得斯听说自己被解雇了，便去见人力资源部的头头。“既然我在公司干了这么久，”他说，“我想至少该给我一封推荐信。”

2 人力资源部主任同意了，并说他第二天就可拿到该信。第二天早上，彼得斯在他的桌子上看一封信，上面写道：“乔纳森·彼得斯在我们公司干了11年。当他离去的时候，我们很满意。”

## 爆笑故事

1 When Peters learned that he was being fired, he went to see the head of human resources. “Since I've been with the firm for so long,” he said, “I think I deserve at least a letter of recommendation.”

2 The human resources director agreed and said he'd have the letter the next day. The following morning, Peters found a letter on his desk. It read, “Jonathan Peters worked for our company for 11 years. When he left us, we were very satisfied.”

## 生词宝库

fire [ˈfaɪə] *v.* 解雇

human resources 人力资源

firm [fɜːm] *n.* 公司

deserve [dɪˈzɜːv] *v.* 应受；值得

recommendation [ˌrekəmenˈdeɪʃn] *n.* 推荐信

company [ˈkʌmpənɪ] *n.* 公司

# Two Hunters
# 两个猎人

1 Once two hunters went hunting in the forest. One of them suddenly fell down by accident. He showed the whites of his eyes and seemed to have ceased breathing.

2 The other hunter soon took out his mobile phone to call the emergency center for help.

3 The operator said calmly, “First, you should make sure that he is already dead.”

4 Then the operator heard a gunshot from the other end of the phone and next he heard the hunter asking, “What should I do next?”

## 点睛译文

1 两个猎人进森林里打猎，其中一个猎人不慎跌倒，两眼翻白，似已停止呼吸。

2 另一个猎人赶紧拿出手机拨通紧急求助电话。

3 接线员沉着地说：“第一步，要先确定你的朋友已经死亡。”

4 于是，接线员在电话里听到一声枪响，然后听到那猎人接着问：“第二步怎办？”

## 生词宝库

hunter [ˈhʌntə] *n.* 猎人
forest [ˈfɒrɪst] *n.* 森林
cease [siːs] *v.* 终止
emergency [ɪˈmɜːdʒənsɪ] *n.* 紧急情况
calmly [ˈkɑːmlɪ] *adv.* 冷静地

# A Smart Horse

# 聪明的马

## 点睛译文

1 一位农夫在犁田时，不慎跌倒摔伤了屁股，他的马立即飞奔到5里外最近的小镇，载了一位医生回来。

2 一个朋友看到后便夸赞说：“你这匹马真是聪明！”

3 农夫说：“也没有你想得那么聪明啦！它带来的是一位兽医！”

## 爆笑故事

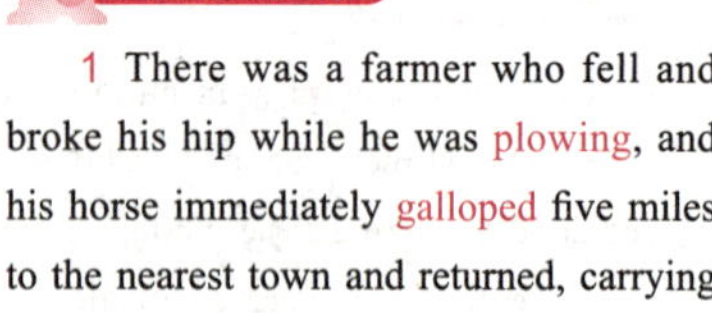

1 There was a farmer who fell and broke his hip while he was plowing, and his horse immediately galloped five miles to the nearest town and returned, carrying a doctor on his back.

2 “That’s a pretty smart horse,” the farmer’s friend later observed.

3 “Well, he’s not really so smart,” the farmer said, “The doctor he brought back was a veterinarian!”

## 生词宝库

plow [plaʊ] v. 耕犁

gallop [ˈgæləp] v. 飞驰

observe [əbˈzɜːv] v. 看到

veterinarian [ˌvetərɪˈneərɪən] n. 兽医

# Tightfisted Till the End

# 本性难移

## 爆笑故事

1 When a very miserly man nicknamed the "stingy ghost" died and went to hell, the Yama King reproached him, saying, "You stingy ghost! When you were alive, you clung hard to everything and wouldn't give to anyone. Even when you saw others in poverty and misery, you refused to offer them help. Also, you didn't take good care of your parents, relatives or friends and let them suffer and starve. For your evil karma, you'll be dumped into a pot of boiling oil."

2 The ghost wardens then escorted the man to the pot of boiling oil, and when they arrived, he looked at the pot and said, "Hey! Wait a minute! There's so much oil in it. What a waste! Please drain out the oil, sell it and give me the money. Then, you can simply dump me in a pot of boiling water! There's no need for oil. You're using too much oil to cook one person anyway!"

## 点睛译文

1 有一个人很吝啬，叫"吝啬鬼"，他死了以后下地狱，阎罗王骂他说："你这个吝啬鬼，在人世间的时候，什么东西都紧抓不放，什么人都不给，看到贫穷、痛苦的人也不帮助，父母、亲戚、朋友也没有照顾好，让他们都挨饿受苦，你这种凶恶的业障，应该被放入滚开的油锅里面。"

2 鬼差就带他到滚得很热、很烫的油锅那边，吝啬鬼一看就说："喔，等一下！油那么多，怎么那么浪费呢？你们先把这些油倒出来，卖出去后把钱给我，然后丢我在热烫的水里就可以了！何必用油，而且还用那么多油，不就煮一个人嘛！"

## 生词宝库

miserly [ˈmaɪzəlɪ] *adj.* 吝啬的

nickname [ˈnɪkneɪm] *v.* 给……取绰号

stingy [ˈstɪndʒɪ] *adj.* 吝啬的

reproach [rɪˈprəʊtʃ] *v.* 责备

cling [klɪŋ] *v.* 坚持；紧握

misery [ˈmɪzərɪ] *n.* 痛苦

relative [ˈrelətɪv] *n.* 亲戚

oil [ɒɪl] *n.* 油

escort [ˈeskɔːt] *v.* 护送；陪同

pot [pɒt] *n.* 锅

# Is He Really Ill

# 他真病了吗

## 爆笑故事

1 On a hot summer day an elderly gentleman faints in the street. A small crowd immediately gathers around him.

2 "Give the poor man a glass of brandy." advises a woman.

3 "Give him a heart massage." says someone else.

4 "No, just give him some brandy." insists the woman.

5 "Call an ambulance." yells another person.

6 "A brandy!"

7 The man suddenly sits up and exclaims, "Shut up, everybody, and do as the kind lady says!"

## 点睛译文

1 在一个炎热的夏天，一位上了年纪的男子昏倒在街头。一群人立刻围了上去。

2 "给这个可怜的人一杯白兰地吧。"一位女士建议。

3 "给他施行心脏按压，进行急救。"另外一个人说。

4 "不，还是给他一些白兰地。"那位女士坚持说。

5 "还是叫一辆救护车吧。"有人叫道。

6 "一杯白兰地。"

7 这时地上的那个人坐了起来，嚷着："都闭嘴，就照那位好心的太太说的去做！"

## 生词宝库

faint [feɪnt] *v.* 昏倒
brandy [ˈbrændɪ] *n.* 白兰地
advise [ədˈvaɪz] *v.* 建议
massage [ˈmæsɑːʒ] *v.* 按摩
insist [ɪnˈsɪst] *v.* 坚持
ambulance [ˈæmbjʊləns] *n.* 救护车

# Good News and Bad News
# 好消息和坏消息

## 爆笑故事

1 The soldiers had been marching and fighting, they were dirty, hot and tired. One day, the general announced: "My men, I have some good news and some bad news for you. Which one would you like first?"

2 "The good news!" they all shouted.

3 "OK," said the General. "The good news is that you will each be receiving a complete change of clothing."

4 "Hurrah!" chorused the soldiers.

5 "And now for the bad news. Jack, you will change with John. John, you will change with Tom. Tom, you will change with Robert. Robert ..."

## 点睛译文

1 士兵们连续地行军、作战，他们又累又热又脏。一天，将军宣布："士兵们，我有一些好消息和坏消息要告诉你们。你们要先听哪个呢？"

2 "好消息！"他们嚷道。

3 "好吧，"将军说，"好消息就是你们每个人都可以彻底地换一身衣服。"

4 "好呀！"士兵们高兴地大叫起来。

5 "现在呢，该是坏消息了。杰克，你将和约翰换衣服。约翰，你和汤姆换。汤姆，你和罗伯特换，罗伯特……"

## 生词宝库

march [mɑːtʃ] *v.* 行军

general [ˈdʒenərəl] *n.* 将军

complete [kəmˈpliːt] *adj.* 彻底的

chorus [ˈkɔːrəs] *v.* 一齐说，异口同声地说

# I Need Your Football
# 我需要你的足球

## 爆笑故事

1 George knocked on the door of his friend's house. When his friend's mother answered he asked, "Can Albert come out to play?"

2 "No," said the mother, "It's too cold."

3 "Well, then," said George, "Can his football come out to play?"

## 点睛译文

1 乔治敲着他朋友家的门。当朋友的妈妈来应门时，他问："阿尔伯特可以出来玩吗？"

2 "不行，"那位妈妈说，"天气太冷了。"

3 "噢，那么，"乔治说，"那他的足球可以出来玩吗？"

## 生词宝库

door [dɔː] *n.* 门

house [haʊs] *n.* 房子

come out 出来

# One More Pie
# 还有一块馅饼

1 一个老妇人因为小男孩带来的礼物感到很是高兴。

2 “明天我将要去拜访你妈妈，”她说，“对她这个可爱的馅饼表示感谢。”

3 “嗯，如果你不介意的话，”男孩儿紧张地说，“你能不能感谢她的两块儿馅饼呢？”

1 The old lady was delighted with the gift the boy had brought her.

2 “I'll go round and see your mother tomorrow,” she said, “And I'll thank her for this lovely pie.”

3 “Um, if you don't mind,” the boy said nervously, “could you thank her for two pies?”

## 生词宝库

lovely [ˈlʌvlɪ] *adj.* 可爱的

pie [paɪ] *n.* 馅饼

mind [maɪnd] *v.* 介意

# One Big Happy Family
# 快乐大家庭

1 The warden of the prison felt sorry for one of his inmates because every weekend on Visitor's Day, most of the prisoners had family members and friends coming, but poor George always sat alone in his cell.

2 So one Visitor's Day, the warden called George to his office and said, "I notice you've never had any visitors, George." Sympathetically, he put his hand on George's shoulder. "Tell me, don't you have any friends or family?"

3 George replied, "Oh, sure I do, Warden. It's just that they're all in here!"

点睛译文

1 典狱长对狱中一位囚犯深感同情，因为每逢周末的探访日，大多数囚犯都有家人或朋友来访，但是可怜的乔治总是孤伶伶地坐在自己的囚室中。

2 因此在一个探访日，典狱长把乔治叫到办公室说："乔治，我注意到从来没有人探望过你。"他满怀同情地把手放在乔治的肩膀上："告诉我，你没有任何朋友或家人吗？"

3 乔治回答："喔！当然有，典狱长，只不过他们全都在这里面！"

生词宝库

warden [ˈwɔːdn] *n.* 看守人
weekend [ˌwiːkˈend] *n.* 周末
alone [əˈləʊn] *adv.* 独自地；单独地
family [ˈfæmɪlɪ] *n.* 家庭；家人

# The Best Stimulant

# 最佳兴奋剂

## 爆笑故事

1 A patient said to his doctor, "Doc, please give me something that will stimulate me, excite me, and put me in a, very, very highly stimulated spirit, a fighting, excited spirit."

2 So the doctor said, "Don't worry, take this, and after you see the bill, you will have all these feelings."

## 点睛译文

1 病人跟医生说："医生，请给我一些可以振奋我、刺激我、让我充满斗志的药，让我能精神异常饱满、亢奋。"

2 医生说："别担心，这个拿去，看到这张帐单以后，你要的这些就都会有了。"

## 生词宝库

stimulate [ˈstɪmjuleɪt] *v.* 激励

excite [ɪkˈsaɪt] *v.* 使激动

fighting [ˈfaɪtɪŋ] *adj.* 战斗的

spirit [ˈspɪrɪt] *n.* 精神

# Ashamed Soldier
# 惭愧的士兵

1 Peter joined the army when he was eighteen, and for several months he was taught how to be a good soldier. He did quite well in everything except shooting.

2 One day he and his friends were practicing their shooting, and all of them were doing quite well except Peter. After he had shot at the target nine times and had not hit it once, the officer who was trying to teach the young soldiers to shoot said, "You're quite hopeless, Peter! Don't waste your last bullet too! Go behind that wall and shoot yourself with it!"

3 Peter felt ashamed. He went behind the wall, and a few seconds later the officer and the other young soldiers heard the sound of a shot.

4 "Heavens!" The officer said, "Has that silly man really shot himself?"

5 He ran behind the wall anxiously,

1 彼得18岁那年参了军，为了成为一名好士兵，他需要参加几个月的学习。彼得在其他方面都做得很好，但是射击不行。

2 一天他和伙伴们练习射击，除了彼得，其他人都没有问题。他射了9次，一次也没有命中目标。这时，教新兵射击的教官说："彼得，你看来是没希望了，不要连最后一发子弹都浪费掉！去那堵墙后面用它向自己打一枪吧。"

3 彼得感到非常惭愧。他走到那堵墙后面。几分钟后，教官和新兵们听到一声枪响。

4 "上帝！"教官叫起来，"难道那个笨蛋真的朝自己开枪了？"

5 他急忙跑到那堵墙后

面，发现彼得安然无恙。“对不起，长官，”他说，“我还是没有命中。”

but Peter was all right. “I’m sorry, sir,” he said, “but I missed again.”

shooting [ˈʃuːtɪŋ] *n.* 射击
hopeless [ˈhəʊplɪs] *adj.* 无希望的
second [ˈsekənd] *n.* 秒
silly [ˈsɪlɪ] *adj.* 愚蠢的

# Alexander the Great

# 亚历山大大帝

## 爆笑故事

1 Landon had made an unsuccessful attempt at the recitation, and the doctor, somewhat nettled, said: "Landon, you don't seem to be getting on very fast in this subject. You seem to lack ambition. Why, at your age Alexander the Great had conquered half the world."

2 "Yes," said Landon, "he couldn't help it, for you will recall the fact, doctor, that Alexander the Great had Aristotle for a teacher."

## 点睛译文

1 兰登作了一次不成功的朗诵。老师有点不悦，对他说道："兰登，你在这门课上好像进步不大，你好像缺乏志向。你怎么了？亚历山大大帝在你这个年龄可已经征服了半个世界了。"

2 "是啊，"兰登说，"他没法不那样。博士先生，您回想一下史实，亚历山大大帝有亚里士多德做他的老师。"

## 生词宝库

unsuccessful [ˌʌnsək'sesfl] *adj.* 不成功的

attempt [ə'tempt] *n.* 尝试

recitation [ˌresɪ'teɪʃn] *n.* 吟诵

somewhat ['sʌmwɒt] *adv.* 稍微

nettle ['netəl] *v.* 惹怒

conquer ['kɒŋkə] *v.* 征服

# Englishman
# 一个英国人

## 点睛译文

1 一天晚上，一个英国人从他住的旅店房间里走出来，来到走廊上，叫旅店的服务员给他拿一杯水来。服务员按他的要求做了。英国人回到了他的房间里，几分钟后他又来到走廊上，让服务员再给他送一杯水。服务员又给他送了一杯水。每隔几分钟，英国人就走出房间重复他的要求。半小时之后，这位感到惊讶的服务员决定问问房客要这些水干什么，英国人不慌不忙地回答："没什么，只不过是我的房间里起火了。"

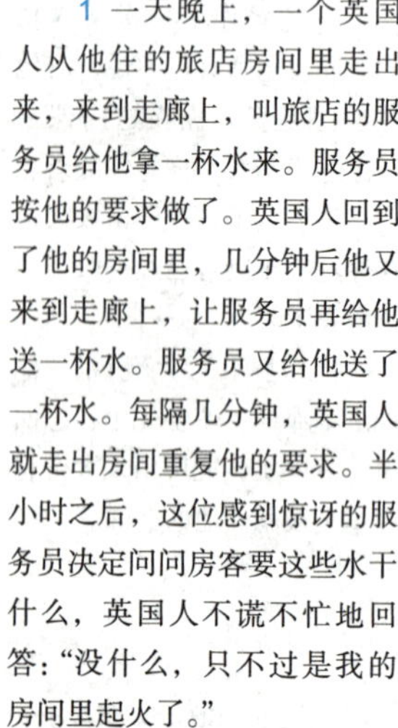

## 爆笑故事

1 Once, late at night, an Englishman came out of his room into the corridor of a hotel and asked the servant to bring him a glass of water. The servant did as he was asked. The Englishman re-entered his room, but a few minutes later he came into the corridor again and once more asked the servant for a glass of water. The servant brought him another glass of water. Every few minutes the Englishmen would come out of his room and repeat his request. After a half-hour the astonished servant decided to ask the Englishman what he was doing with the water. "Nothing." the Englishman answered imperturbably, "It's simply that my room is on fire."

## 点睛译文

corridor [ˈkɒrɪdɔː] *n.* 走廊

request [rɪˈkwest] *n.* 请求

astonished [əˈstɒnɪʃt] *adj.* 惊讶的

imperturbably [ˌɪmpəˌtɜːbəblɪ] *adv.* 平静地；泰然地

# Caught Stealing
# 预算超标的小偷

## 爆笑故事

1 A shoplifter was caught red-handed trying to steal a watch from a jewelry store. "Listen," said the shoplifter, "I know you don't want any trouble either. What do you say I just buy the watch, and we forget about this?"

2 The manager agreed and wrote up the sales slip. The crook looked at the slip and said, "This is a little more than I intended to spend. Can you show me something less expensive?"

## 点睛译文

1 一个小偷在一家珠宝店企图偷走一只手表的时候被当场擒获。"听着，"小偷说，"我知道你们也不想惹麻烦。我把这只表买下，然后我们就当什么也没发生，你看怎样？"

2 经理表示同意，然后填了一张售货单。小偷看着单子说道："这比我最初的预算稍稍高了一点，你们还有没有便宜一点儿的东西。"

## 生词宝库

shoplifter [ˈʃɒplɪftə] *n.* 在商店中行窃的小偷

steal [stiːl] *v.* 偷

jewelry [ˈdʒuːəlrɪ] *n.* 珠宝

crook [krʊk] *n.* < 口 > 小偷

# One Point
# 一分之差

1 位于印第安那州瓦巴西的怀兹中学，其门厅里悬挂着过去40年间篮球队的照片。每幅照片前排中间的队员举着一个篮球，上面标明年份——“62-63”，“63-64”，“64-65”等。

2 一天，我看到一个新生很困惑地看着照片。他朝我转过身来，说道：“多奇怪呀，这些队都是以一分之差输掉的！”

1 The basketball team pictures have been hanging in the hallway at Whites High School in Wabash, Ind., and from the past 40 years. A player in the center of the front row in each picture holds a basketball identifying the year – “62-63”, “63-64”, “64-65”, etc.

2 One day I spotted a freshman looking curiously at the photos. Turning to me, he said, “Isn't it strange how the teams always lost by one point?”

生词宝库

basketball [ˈbɑːskɪtbɔːl] *n.* 篮球
hallway [ˈhɔːlweɪ] *n.* 门厅
freshman [ˈfreʃmən] *n.* 新生
lose [luːz] *v.* 输掉

# An Unwelcome Honor
# 宁可不要的荣耀

1 A doctor came into the hospital ward and said to Mr. Johnson, "I have some good news and some bad news for you."

2 Then Mr. Johnson said, "Please, give me the good news first."

3 So the doctor said, "The doctors here are going to name an incurable disease after you."

1 一位医生走进医院的病房，告诉约翰逊先生："我有一个好消息和一个坏消息要告诉你。"

2 于是，约翰逊先生说道："拜托了，先告诉我好消息吧。"

3 医生说道："本院所有医生决定将以你的名字命名这种无法治愈的疾病。"

## 生词宝库

hospital [ˈhɒspɪtl] *n.* 医院

ward [wɔːd] *n.* 病房

incurable [ɪnˈkjʊərəbl] *adj.* 不能医治的

disease [dɪˈziːz] *n.* 疾病

# Where Does God Live

# 上帝住在哪

1 老师：上帝住哪儿？

2 学生：我想他应该住我家浴室。

3 老师：为什么这么说？

4 学生：因为每天早上我爸都猛敲浴室的大门喊："上帝啊，你怎么还在里面？"

1 Teacher: Where does God live?

2 Student: I think he lives in our bathroom.

3 Teacher: Why do you say that?

4 Student: Well, every morning my daddy bangs on the door and says, "God, are you still in there?"

## 生词宝库

live [lɪv] *v.* 居住

bathroom [ˈbɑːθruːm] *n.* 洗手间

bang [bæŋ] *n.* 巨响

# The Plural Form of Child
# 孩子的复数形式

1 Teacher: What is the plural form of "man", Tom?

2 Tom: Men.

3 Teacher: Good. And the plural form of "child"?

4 Tom: Twins.

1 老师：汤姆，“男人”这个词的复数形式是什么？

2 汤姆：男人们。

3 老师：答得好。那“孩子”的复数形式呢？

4 汤姆：双胞胎。

生词宝库

plural [ˈpluərəl] *adj.* 复数的

form [fɔːm] *n.* 形式

man [mæn] *n.* 男人

child [tʃaɪld] *n.* 小孩

# Do You Miss the School
# 你想念学校吗

1 汤姆昨天没来学校。

2 于是老师问他："汤姆，你昨天没来学校，是不是？"

3 汤姆：（理解为你昨天很想念学校不是吗？）不太想。

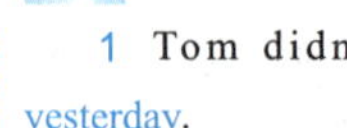


1 Tom didn't come to school yesterday.

2 The teacher says to him, "Tom, you missed school yesterday, didn't you?"

3 Tom: "Not very much!"

生词宝库

school [sku:l] *n.* 学校
yesterday [ˈjestədeɪ] *adv.* 昨天
miss [mɪs] *v.* 想念；错过
much [mʌtʃ] *adv.* 很

# See the Butterfly
# 看蝴蝶

1 One day, Betty saw a man throw a bottle of butter out of the window of his house. He didn't understand why the man did so and when he returned home, he said to his grandma what strange thing the man had done and asked:

2 "Why did the man throw the butter out of the window?"

3 His grandma thought for a while and answered him:

4 "I think he just wanted to see the butterfly."

1 一天，贝蒂看到一个人把一瓶黄油扔到了他房子的窗户外面。他不理解为什么这个人这么做。于是当他回到家里后，他就对他的奶奶讲了那个人所做的奇怪的事情，并问道：

2 “那个人为什么把黄油扔到窗户外面呢？”

3 他的奶奶想了一会儿，回答道：

4 “我想他只是想看蝴蝶了。”

## 生词宝库

throw [θrəʊ] *v.* 扔

butter [ˈbʌtə] *n.* 黄油

strange [streɪndʒ] *adj.* 奇怪的

butterfly [ˈbʌtəflaɪ] *n.* 蝴蝶

# Wings

# 翅膀

1 The fried-chicken restaurant where I was working had a big rush just before closing one day, leaving us with nothing to sell but wings. As I was about to lock the doors, a quietly intoxicated customer came in and ordered dinner. When I asked if wings would be all right, he leaned over the counter and replied, "Lady, I came in here to eat, not fly."

1 一天，我工作的炸鸡店在关门前出现了一阵抢购狂潮，结果除了鸡翅外所有的东西都卖完了。当我正准备锁门时，一名喝醉了的顾客进来要进餐。我问他翅膀行不行，他从柜台上靠过身子来，回答道："女士，我到这儿来是吃东西的，不是要飞！"

rush [rʌʃ] *n.* 抢购

wing [wɪŋ] *n.* 翅膀

intoxicated [ɪnˈtɒksɪkeɪtɪd] *adj.* 喝醉的

counter [ˈkaʊntə] *n.* 柜台

# Save Time
# 拯救时间

1 A: Why did the man put the clock in safe?

2 B: He wanted to save time.

点睛译文

1 A：那个人为什么把钟表放进保险箱？

2 B：他想要拯救时间呀。

clock [klɒk] *n.* 时钟

safe [seɪf] *n.* 保险箱

save [seɪv] *v.* 节省；拯救

time [taɪm] *n.* 时间

# It's Snowing Outside
# 现在外面下着雪

1 汤姆：好消息，老师说今天不管下雨还是天晴（不管什么情况），我们都要考试。

2 约翰：那有什么好高兴的？

3 汤姆：因为现在外面在下雪！

1 Tom: Great news, teacher says that we will have a test today no matter it comes rain or shine.

2 John: So what's great about that?

3 Tom: It's snowing outside!

生词宝库

test [test] *n.* 测试

no matter 无论

shine [ʃaɪn] *v.* 照耀

snow [snəʊ] *v.* 下雪

# How Much Does It Cost to Get Married

# 结婚要花多少钱

## 爆笑故事

1 A little boy asked his father, "Daddy, how much does it cost to get married?"

2 The father replied, "I don't know, son. I'm still paying."

## 点睛译文

1 一个小男孩问他爸爸："爸爸，结婚要花多少钱？"

2 他爸爸回答说："儿子，我还不知道呢，因为我仍在付账（付出代价）。"

## 生词宝库

cost [kɒst] v. 花费

get married 结婚

reply [rɪˈplaɪ] v. 回答

pay [peɪ] v. 支付；付出代价

# My Father's Ashes

# 我父亲的灰

## 点睛译文

1 某人第一次去女孩子家，女孩将他带到客厅后便去厨房找喝的东西。他独自站在客厅里，看到壁炉架上放着一只精巧的花瓶，便拿起来看，这时女孩走进来了。

2 “这是什么？”他问。

3 “哦，里面放着我父亲的灰。”女孩说。

4 “哦……我……真不知道该说些什么。”这人说道。

5 “是的，确实令人不敢相信，”女孩说，“父亲每次都懒得去厨房拿烟灰缸。”

## 爆笑故事

1 A guy goes to a girl's house for the first time and she shows him into the living room. She excuses herself to go to the kitchen to make them a few drinks and as he's standing there alone, he notices a cute little vase on the mantelpiece. He picks it up and as he's looking at it, she walks back in.

2 "What's this?" he says.

3 "Oh," she says, "my father's ashes are in there."

4 "Ooops... I... don't know what to say," says the guy.

5 "Yeah I know, it's shocking," says the girl. "He's too lazy to go to the kitchen to get an ashtray."

## 生词宝库

excuse [ɪk'skjuːs] *v.* 原谅

cute [kjuːt] *adj.* 可爱的；漂亮的

mantelpiece ['mæntlpiːs] *n.* 壁炉台

ashtray ['æʃtreɪ] *n.* 烟灰缸

# A Pair of Socks
# 一双袜子

1 A cop spotted a woman driving and knitting at the same time. Coming up beside her, he said, "Pull over!"

2 "No," she replied, "a pair of socks!"

点睛译文

1 巡警发现一名妇女边开车边织毛衣，便开车上前，说："靠边停车（pull over 也表示套头衫）！"

2 "不，"她回答，"是一双袜子！"

生词宝库

cop [kɒp] *n.* 警察

drive [draɪv] *v.* 开车

knit [nɪt] *v.* 编织

sock [sɒk] *n.* 短袜

# Pig or Witch
# 猪还是女巫

## 点睛译文

1 一个男人在一条陡峭狭窄的山路上驾车，一个女人从同一个方向驾车而来。他们相遇时，那个女的从窗中伸出头来叫到：“猪！”

2 那个男的立即从窗中伸出头来回敬道：“女巫！！”

3 他们继续前行。这个男的在下一个路口转弯时，撞上了路中间的一头猪。

4 要是这个男的能听懂那个女人的意思就好了。

## 爆笑故事

1 A man is driving up a steep, narrow mountain road. A woman is driving down the same road. As they pass each other, the woman leans out of the window and yells "Pig!"

2 The man immediately leans out of his window and replies, "Witch!!"

3 They each continue on their way, and as the man rounds the next corner, he crashes into a pig in the middle of the road.

4 If only men would listen.

## 生词宝库

steep [stiːp] *adj.* 陡峭的

witch [wɪtʃ] *n.* 女巫

corner [ˈkɔːnə] *n.* 角落

crash [kræʃ] *v.* 撞上

# Right
# 右还是对

## 爆笑故事

1 An overseas student in America wanted to take the test of the international driver's license. Because he was too nervous at the examination, he saw the ground line is "turn left".

2 He turned to ask the official, "Turn left?"

3 The official answered, "Right."

4 So he immediately turned to the right...

## 点睛译文

1 一位在美的留学生，想要考国际驾照。在考试时因为过于紧张，看到地上标线是"向左"。

2 他转向考官问道："向左转吗？"

3 考官回答："是的（right也表示右边）"。

4 于是他立刻向右转了……

## 生词宝库

overseas [ˌəuvəˈsiːz] *adj.* 海外的

license [ˈlaɪsns] *n.* 执照

ground [graʊnd] *n.* 地面

official [əˈfɪʃl] *n.* 官员

# One Side of the Case
# 一面之辞

1 一位法官问我们这群陪审员候选人是否有人应当免权。一个人举起了手。

2 “我的左耳听不见。”那人告诉法官。

3 “你右边的耳朵听得见吗？”法官问道。那人点了点头。

4 “你将被允许加入陪审团。”法官宣布，“我们每次只听一面之辞。”

1 A judge asked our group of potential jurors whether anyone should be excused, and one man raised his hand.

2 “I can’t hear out of my left ear.” the man told the judge.

3 “Can you hear out of your right ear?” the judge asked. The man nodded his head.

4 “You’ll be allowed to serve on the jury.” the judge declared. “We only listen to one side of the case at a time.”

**生词宝库**

potential [pə'tenʃl] *adj.* 潜在的，可能的

juror ['dʒʊərə] *n.* 陪审员

raise [reɪz] *v.* 举高

ear [ɪə] *n.* 耳朵

case [keɪs] *n.* 案例

# Who Is Closer

# 谁更亲近

1 Teacher: Who is closer to you, your mom or your dad?

2 Tom: Mom is closer, because dad is farther.

1 老师：爸爸和妈妈谁和你更亲？

2 汤姆：妈妈更亲，因为爸爸更远。

## 生词宝库

closer ['kləuzə] *adj.* 更近的

mom [mɒm] *n.* 妈妈

dad [dæd] *n.* 爸爸

farther ['fɑːðə] *adj.* 更远的（与 father 同音）

# Imitation

# 模仿

## 点睛译文

1 一个男孩放学回家时，觉得肚子痛。“来，坐下，吃点点心，”妈妈说，“你肚子痛是因为肚子是空的。吃点东西就会好的。”

2 一会儿，男孩的爸爸下班回家了，说自己头痛。

3 “你头痛是因为你的脑袋是空的，”他那聪明的儿子说，“装点东西在里面，就会好的。”

## 爆笑故事

1 A schoolboy went home with a pain in his stomach. “Well, sit down and eat your tea,” said his mother. “Your stomach's hurting because it's empty. It'll be all right when you've got something in it.”

2 Shortly afterwards Dad come in from the office, complaining of a headache.

3 “That's because it's empty,” said his bright son. “You'd be all right if you had something in it.”

## 生词宝库

pain [peɪn] *n.* 疼痛

afterwards [ˈɑːftəwədz] *adv.* 后来

headache [ˈhedeɪk] *n.* 头痛

bright [braɪt] *adj.* 聪明的

# The Sons
# 儿子们

## 爆笑故事

1 The mothers of four priests got together and were discussing their sons.

2 "My son is a monsignor," said the first proud woman. "When he enters a room, people say, 'Hello, Monsignor'."

3 The second mother went on, "My son is a bishop. When he enters a room, people say, 'Hello, Your Excellency'."

4 "My son is a cardinal." continued the next one. "When he enters a room, people say, 'Hello, Your Eminence'."

5 The fourth mother thought for a moment. "My son is six-foot-ten and weighs 300 pounds." she said, "When he enters a room, people say, 'Oh, my God'!"

## 点睛译文

1 4位牧师的母亲聚到一起谈论她们的儿子。

2 "我的儿子是个教士。"第一位母亲自豪地说道，"他进入房间，人们都说，'您好，阁下'。"

3 第二位母亲说："我的儿子是位主教。他进入房间，人们都称，'您好，大人'。"

4 "我的儿子是位红衣主教。"第三位母亲接着说，"他走进房间，人们都说，'您好，尊敬的主教大人'。"

5 第四位母亲略思片刻。"我的儿子身高6英尺10，体重300磅。"她说，"他要是走入房间，人们都说'哦，我的上帝'！"

## 生词宝库

priest [priːst] *n.* 教士

monsignor [mɒnˈsiːnjə] *n.* 阁下（对罗马天主教大主教的称呼）

bishop [ˈbɪʃəp] *n.* 主教

cardinal [ˈkɑːdɪnəl] *n.* 红衣主教

eminence [ˈemɪnəns] *n.* 崇高

# March
# 三月

## 点睛译文

1 老师：当兵的不喜欢几月份？

2 学生：3 月。

3 老师：你是怎么想的？

4 学生：因为士兵讨厌行军呀。

## 爆笑故事

1 Teacher: What month do soldiers hate?

2 Student: March.

3 Teacher: Why do you think so?

4 Student: Because soldiers hate march.

## 生词宝库

month [mʌnθ] *n.* 月

soldier [ˈsəʊldʒə] *n.* 士兵

hate [heɪt] *v.* 厌恶

march [mɑːtʃ] *n.* 行军；三月（首字母大写）

# They're All Drowned
# 他们全都淹死了

1 The great painter was asked, one day to paint a picture of Pharaoh Crossing the Red Sea. A little while after the picture had been commenced, a hitch arose over the fee, and Hogarth found that he would have to complete the commission for about half the sum he expected. When the work was completed, the patron was asked to come and inspect it. As a matter of fact, the picture was just one daub of brilliant red.

2 "What's this?" exclaimed the purchaser. "I asked for the Red Sea, on the occasion of the celebrated passage."

3 "That's it." replied Hogarth.

4 "But, where are the Israelites?"

5 "They are all gone over."

6 "Where are the Egyptians?"

7 "They're all drowned."

1 一天，有人请了位伟大的画家画一幅《法老渡红海图》。这幅画在刚开始创作不久，就在酬金方面出现了问题。霍格思发现，完成这幅画后，他只能得到他想要的大约一半的钱。当作品完成之后，那位主顾被请来看画。只见那幅画是胡乱涂抹的一片鲜红。

2 "这是什么？"那位买主喊了起来。"我要的是红海，是那次著名的航海。"

3 "这就是，"霍格思回答说。

4 "可是以色列人在哪儿？"

5 "他们都已经渡过去了。"

6 "埃及人在哪儿？"

7 "他们全都淹死了。"

## 生词宝库

painter [ˈpeɪntə] *n.* 画家

commence [kəˈmens] *v.* 开始

hitch [hɪtʃ] *n.* 妨碍

commission [kəˈmɪʃən] *n.* 委任；委托

daub [dɔːb] *n.* 涂抹；拙劣的画

occasion [əˈkeɪʒən] *n.* 场合

Egyptian [ɪˈdʒɪpʃn] *n.* 埃及人

drown [draʊn] *v.* 淹死

# How Many Feet Are There in a Yard

# 院子里有多少只脚

## 爆笑故事

1 Teacher: How many feet are there in a yard?

2 Student: It depends on how many people stand in the yard.

3 Teacher: Why?

4 Student: One has two feet, so you can count.

## 点睛译文

1 老师：一码有多少英尺？

2 学生：这要看院子里站了多少人。

3 老师：为什么？

4 学生：一个人两只脚，这样你就可以计算了。

## 生词宝库

feet [fiːt] *n.* 英尺；脚（foot的复数）

yard [jɑːd] *n.* 码

stand [stænd] *v.* 站立

count [kaʊnt] *v.* 计算

# Lose His Appetite
# 没胃口

1 在一次晚餐聚会上，一位腼腆的年青人一直在冥思苦想对女主人说一些好听的话。

2 机会终于来了，女主人转向他说："琼斯先生，您今晚的饭量太小了。"

3 "坐在您身边，"他殷勤地说道，"任何男人都会失去胃口的。"

1 At a dinner party a shy young man had been trying to think of something nice to say to his hostess.

2 At last he saw his chance when she turned to him and remarked, "What a small appetite you have tonight, Mr. Jones."

3 "To sit next to you," he replied gallantly, "would cause any man to lose his appetite."

生词宝库

shy [ʃaɪ] *adj.* 腼腆的

hostess [ˈhəʊstəs] *n.* 女主人

remark [rɪˈmɑːk] *v.* 评论

appetite [ˈæpɪtaɪt] *n.* 食欲

gallantly [ˈɡæləntlɪ] *adv.* 献殷勤地

# The Poor Man
# 可怜的人

## 爆笑故事

1 “Oh, my poor man.” exclaimed the kind old lady, “It must be dreadful to be lame. But it would be much worse if you were blind.”

2 “You’re absolutely right,” said the beggar, obviously an old hand at the game. “When I was blind, people kept giving me foreign coins.”

## 点睛译文

1 “啊，可怜的人！”善良的老妇人惊叹道，“脚瘸就够惨的了，要是眼瞎就更糟了。”

2 “你说的一点儿没错。”那乞丐说。他显然是乞讨老手。“我眼瞎的时候，人们老是给我外币。”

## 生词宝库

poor [pʊə] *adj.* 可怜的；贫穷的

dreadful [ˈdredfl] *adj.* 可怕的

lame [leɪm] *adj.* 跛足的

beggar [ˈbegə] *n.* 乞丐

coin [kɒɪn] *n.* 硬币

# Ten to One

# 10比1

1 Mom: What's the most difficult train to catch?

2 Son: The 12:50 train, because it's ten to one if you catch it.

1 妈妈：赶什么火车最不容易？

2 儿子：是12点50分的火车，因为赶上它只有10比1的概率。（原文可理解为一点差十分）

## 生词宝库

most [məʊst] *adv.* 最

difficult [ˈdɪfɪkəlt] *adj.* 困难的

train [treɪn] *n.* 火车

catch [kætʃ] *v.* 赶上

# Dumas
# 仲马

## 爆笑故事

1 One day a man was taunting Alexander Dumas, the great French novelist, with his ancestry.

2 "Why," snarled the fellow, "you are a quadroon; your father was a mulatto, and your grandfather was a negro."

3 "Yes." roared Dumas, "and if you wish to know, my great grandfather was a monkey. In fact, my pedigree began where yours terminates."

## 点睛译文

1 有一天，一个人在嘲弄法国伟大小说家亚历山大·仲马，讥笑他的祖先。

2 那家伙厉声说："唔，你是四分之一黑白混血儿，你父亲是黑白混血儿，而你的祖父是个黑人。"

3 "是的，"仲马大声回敬，"还有呢，如果你想知道的话，我的曾祖父是一只猴子。其实我的血统起始于你的血统终止的地方。"

## 生词宝库

taunt [tɔ:nt] *v.* 嘲弄

novelist ['nɒvəlɪst] *n.* 小说家

ancestry ['ænsestrɪ] *n.* 祖先

snarl [snɑ:l] *v.* 咆哮；怒骂

quadroon [kwɒd'ru:n] *n.* 夸德隆（有四分之一黑人血统的人）

mulatto [mju:'lætəʊ] *n.* 白黑混血儿

negro ['ni:grəʊ] *n.* 黑人

pedigree ['pedɪgri:] *n.* 血统

terminate ['tɜ:mɪneɪt] *v.* 终止

# Go to Bed

# 睡觉

1 问：人们为什么睡觉（go to bed 也可理解为“走向床”）？

2 答：因为床不会走向我们。

1 Q: Why do people go to bed?

2 A: Because the bed won't come to us.

## 生词宝库

why [waɪ] *adv.* 为什么

bed [bed] *n.* 床

us [əs] *pron.* 我们

# Fall and Fall Asleep
# 摔跤和睡觉

## 爆笑故事

1 Betty: I fell last night, unconscious for eight hours.

2 Hetty: How dreadful! Where did you fall?

3 Betty: I fell asleep.

## 点睛译文

1 贝蒂：我昨晚摔了一跤，昏迷了8个小时。

2 赫蒂：真可怕！你在哪里摔的?

3 贝蒂：我是在睡梦中。

## 生词宝库

fall [fɔːl] *v.* 倒下；进入某种状态

unconscious [ʌnˈkɒnʃəs] *adj.* 失去知觉的

dreadful [ˈdredfl] *adj.* 可怕的

fall asleep 睡觉

# Knights & Nights
# 黑暗时代

点睛译文

1 老师：为什么有时我们会称中世纪为黑暗时代呢？

2 贝蒂：因为那时有许多骑士。

爆笑故事

1 Teacher: Why do we sometimes call the Middle Ages the Dark Ages?

2 Betty: Because they had so many knights.

生词宝库

sometimes [ˈsʌmtaɪmz] *adv.* 有时

Middle age 中世纪

dark [dɑːk] *adj.* 黑暗的

knight [naɪt] *n.* 骑士（与night谐音）

# Trouble with Propositions
## 介词问题

1 A new student was just finding his way around Harvard University.

2 “Excuse me,” he asked an upperclassman, “can you tell me where the library’ s at?”

3 “What appalling diction,” sneered the older student. “I can’t imagine how you could have been admitted to Harvard. Don’t you know better than to end a sentence with a preposition?”

4 “OK. Can you tell me where the library’s at, asshole?”

1 一位哈佛大学新生正在熟悉校园环境。

2 “对不起，”他问一位高年级学长，“您能告诉我图书馆在哪里吗？”

3 “好可怕的用字喔！”那名学长嘲弄他道，“不知道你这位老弟是怎么获准进入哈佛的。难道你不知道介词不要放在一个句子后面吗？”

4 “好吧！你能告诉我图书馆在哪里吗，驴蛋？”

### 生词宝库

upperclassman [ˌʌpəˈklɑːsmən] *n.* 高年级学生

appalling [əˈpɔːlɪŋ] *adj.* 可怕的

preposition [ˌprepəˈzɪʃn] *n.* 介词

asshole [ˈæshəʊl] *n.* 讨厌的人

# Blue Jeans
# 蓝色牛仔服

1 问：什么衣服总是伤感的？

2 答：蓝色牛仔服。

1 Q: What clothing is always sad?

2 A: Blue Jeans.

clothing [ˈkləʊðɪŋ] *n.* 衣服

sad [sæd] *adj.* 伤心的

blue [bluː] *adj.* 蓝色的；忧郁的

jeans [dʒiːnz] *n.* 牛仔裤

# A Friend in Need
# 需要帮助的朋友

1 Q: Who will be your real friend, a poor friend or a rich one?

2 A: A poor friend.

3 Q: Why?

4 A: Because a friend in need is a friend indeed.

1 问：贫穷的朋友和富有的朋友，谁会成为你真正的朋友？

2 答：贫穷的朋友。

3 问：为什么？

4 答：因为需要帮助的朋友才是真朋友（患难见真情）。

## 生词宝库

real [rɪəl] adj 真正的

poor [puə] *adj.* 贫穷的

rich [rɪtʃ] *adj.* 富有的

indeed [ɪn'di:d] *adv.* 真正地

# Santa's True Profession

# 圣诞老人的真实职业

1 圣诞老人的真实职业是什么？

2 考虑以下几点：

3 1. 你其实从来没见过圣诞老人，你看见的都是他的助手。

4 2. 圣诞老人不想退休，就可以一直当他的圣诞老人。

5 3. 圣诞老人不会做实事，他都是指挥一堆帮手帮他做完所有的事情，但是事情做得好还是不好，功绩和责任都算圣诞老人的。

6 4. 圣诞老人实行的可不是朝九晚五双休制。

7 5. 圣诞老人经常旅行。

8 圣诞老人显然是一个高级职员！

1 Do You Know Santa's True Profession?

2 Consider the following:

3 1. You never actually see Santa, only his "assistants."

4 2. Santa keeps his job until he decides to retire.

5 3. Santa doesn't really do the work; he directs a bunch of helpers to do all his work for him, but he's the one who everybody credits with the work.

6 4. Santa doesn't work a 40-hour week.

7 5. Santa travels a lot.

8 Santa is obviously a senior faculty member with tenure!

## 生词宝库

Santa [ˈsæntə] *n.* 圣诞老人

profession [prəˈfeʃn] *n.* 职业

following [ˈfɒləʊɪŋ] *n.* 下列事物

bunch [bʌntʃ] *n.* 群

travel [ˈtrævl] *v.* 旅行

faculty [ˈfækltɪ] *n.*（某一专门行业的）全体从业人员

tenure [ˈtenjə] *n.* 占有权；任期

# Pear and Pair
# 梨和一对

## 点睛译文

1 问：什么水果永远不会是单个的？

2 答：是梨。

## 爆笑故事

1 Q: What fruit is never found singly?

2 A: A pear.

## 生词宝库

fruit [fruːt] *n.* 水果

found [faʊnd] *v.* 发现（动词 find 的过去分词）

singly [ˈsɪŋglɪ] *adv.* 单独地

pear [peə] *n.* 梨（与 pair 谐音）

# The Piggy in the Refrigerator

# 冰箱里的储蓄罐

1 My cousin always "borrows" money from her older brother's piggy bank, which drives him crazy.

2 One day, she found the piggy in, of all places, the refrigerator.

3 Inside was this note: "Dear sister, I hope you'll understand, but my capital has been frozen."

1 我表妹总是从她哥哥的小猪存钱罐里"借钱"，她哥哥对此事感到很愤怒。

2 一天，表妹四处寻找，最后竟然在冰箱里发现了存钱罐。

3 存钱罐里有张纸条："亲爱的妹妹，我希望你能够理解，我的资产现在已被冻结。"

**生词宝库**

piggy [ˈpɪɡɪ] *n.* 小猪

refrigerator [rɪˈfrɪdʒəreɪtə] *n.* 冰箱

understand [ʌndəˈstænd] *v.* 理解

capital [ˈkæpɪtl] *n.* 资产

# The Letter E
# 字母E

1 问：大多数人最害怕什么字母？

2 答：是字母 E。

3 问：为什么？

4 答：因为它是生命的结束。

1 Q: Which letter does most people fear most?

2 A: The letter E.

3 Q: Why?

4 A: Because it's the end of life.

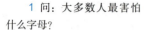

## 生词宝库

letter [ˈletə] *n.* 字母

most [məʊst] *adj.* 大多数的

fear [fɪə] *v.* 害怕

end [end] *n.* 结束

# Post Office
# 邮局

## 爆笑故事

1 A: Do you know what two words contain thousands of letters?

2 B: Post Office.

3 A: How do you think so?

4 B: Yes, of course. There are thousands of letters in the post office.

## 点睛译文

1 A: 哪两个单词包含了所有的字母？

2 B: 邮局。

3 A: 你为什么这么认为？

4 B：当然是了。邮局里有成千上万封信。

## 生词宝库

contain [kənˈteɪn] *v.* 包含

thousands [ˈθaʊzndz] *n.* 数千的

letter [ˈletə] *n.* 信件；字母

of course 当然

# Just Friends
# 只是朋友

## 点睛译文

1 为了寻找停车位，我开着车在停车场饶了一圈又一圈。还是没找到。然后我注意到一男一女朝我走了过来。

2 “出来了？” 我向他们问道。

3 “不，” 那个男人说，“只是朋友。”

## 爆笑故事

1 I was driving around and around a parking garage in search for an available spot. But I found nothing. Then I noticed a couple walking towards me.

2 “Going out?” I called to them.

3 “No,” said the man, “just friends.”

## 生词宝库

parking [ˈpɑːkɪŋ] *adj.* 停车的

garage [ˈɡærɑːʒ] *n.* 车库

available [əˈveɪləbl] *adj.* 可利用的

towards [təˈwɔːdz] prep. 向，朝

go out 相恋；出去

# A Life for a Life
# 以“命”抵命

1 The English author, Richard Savage, was once living in London in great poverty. In order to earn a little money he had written the story of his life, but not many copies of the book had been sold in the shops, and Savage was living from hand to mouth. As a result of his lack of food he became very ill, but after a time, owing to the skill of the doctor who had looked after him, he got well again.

2 After a week or two the doctor sent a bill to Savage for his visits, but poor Savage hadn't any money and couldn't pay it. The doctor waited for another month and sent the bill again. But still no money came. After several weeks he sent it to him again asking for his money.

3 In the end he came to Savage's house and asked him for payment, saying to Savage, "You know you owe your life to me and expected some gratitude from you." "I agree." said Savage, "that I owe

点睛译文

1 英国作家理查德·萨维奇一度在伦敦过着贫困潦倒的生活，为了赚几个钱，他曾写了有关他自己的生平事迹。但是这部书在书店里并没有卖出几本，萨维奇过着朝不保夕的日子。由于缺乏食物，他病得很厉害。后来，由于给他治疗的那个医生医术高明，他才又恢复了健康。

2 过了一两个星期之后，医生给萨维奇送来了一张讨要诊费的账单，但是贫穷的萨维奇没有钱来偿付。医生等了一个月后又送来了账单，但仍然未索回分文。几个星期之后，他又送来账单要钱。

3 最后，医生本人来到了萨维奇的家中，对他说：“你明白，你是欠我一条命的，我希望你有所报答。”“是的。”萨维奇说，“我是欠你一条命，为了向你证明我不是不报答你的诊治之恩，我将把我的命给你。”说着这番话，萨维奇递给医生两卷书，名叫《理查德·萨维奇的一生》。

my life to you, and to prove to you that I am not ungrateful for your work I will give my life to you.” With these words he handed to him two volumes entitled, *The life of Richard Savage.*

## 生词宝库

author [ˈɔːθə] *n.* 作者；作家
poverty [ˈpɒvətɪ] *n.* 贫困
life [laɪf] *n.* 生命；一生
bill [bɪl] *n.* 账单
payment [ˈpeɪmənt] *n.* 支付
owe [əʊ] *v.* 欠
gratitude [ˈgrætɪtjuːd] *n.* 感谢；感激
ungrateful [ʌnˈgreɪtfl] *adj.* 忘恩负义的
volume [ˈvɒljuːm] *n.* 卷；册
entitle [ɪnˈtaɪtəl] *v.* 定名为……

# What Comes Before Six

# 6前面是什么

1 A mother asked his son, "What comes before six?"

2 The son thought for a while and answered, "The milkman."

3 The mother was confused and angry, said, "what do you learn at school?"

4 The little son cried and said, "you told me that the milkman comes at six."

1 一个妈妈问儿子："6前面是什么？"

2 儿子想了一会儿回答说："送牛奶的人。"

3 母亲摸不着头脑又很生气，说道"你在学校都学了什么？"

4 儿子哭着说："是你告诉我说送牛奶的人6点钟之前来。"

## 生词宝库

before [bɪˈfɔː] pref. 在……之前

while [waɪl] *n.* 一会儿

milkman [ˈmɪlkmən] *n.* 送牛奶的人

confused [kənˈfjuːzd] *adj.* 困惑的

# A Wrong Email
# 一封发错的邮件

## 点睛译文

1 一个伊利诺伊州的男人离开已经开始下雪的芝加哥，要去南方的福罗里达州度假。他的太太也正好在福罗里达出差，准备第二天跟他碰面。他到了酒店之后，打算先给她太太发一封邮件。

2 因为找不到记着他太太邮件地址的那张纸条，所以他决定凭记忆发出这封信。可惜，他在输入地址的时候漏掉了一个字母，因而把这封邮件发到了另一位夫人的邮箱里，这位夫人的牧师丈夫头天才刚刚过世。这个悲伤的寡妇打开邮箱，读完信后哀嚎一声、倒在地板上就死了。

3 她的家人闻声赶来，发现电脑屏幕上留着这么一封信：

4 亲爱的老婆：

5 我刚刚住进来，一切

## 爆笑故事

1 An Illinois man left the snowballed streets of Chicago for a vacation in Florida. His wife was on a business trip and was planning to meet him there the next day. When he reached his hotel, he decided to send his wife a quick e-mail.

2 Unable to find the scrap of paper on which he had written her e-mail address, he did his best to type it in from memory. Unfortunately, he missed one letter, and his note was directed instead to an elderly preacher's wife whose husband had passed away only the day before. When the grieving widow checked her e-mail, she took one look at the monitor, let out a piercing scream, and fell to the floor dead.

3 At the sound, her family rushed into the room and saw this note on the screen:

4 Dearest Wife,

5 Just got checked in. Everything

prepared for your arrival tomorrow.

6 Your Loving Husband.

7 P.S. Sure is hot down here.

都准备好了，就等你来。

6 你亲爱的老公。

7 另：这下面还真是热。

## 生词宝库

snowball ['snəʊbɔːl] *v.* 滚雪球般扩大

vacation [və'keɪʃən] *n.* 假期

scrap [skræp] *n.* 碎片；纸片

type [taɪp] *v.* 打字

memory ['memərɪ] *n.* 记忆

monitor ['mɒnɪtə] *n.* 显示器

piercing ['pɪəsɪŋ] *adj.* 尖锐的